Organ-isms

Organ-isms

Anecdotes from the world of the King of Instruments

compiled and written by

Jenny Setchell

with a foreword by Dame Gillian Weir

Illustrations by Terence Dobson

Organ-isms

First published 2008

Reprinted 2009

This edition printed in England

by CopyTECH (UK) Limited

book@nzorgan.com

ISBN 978-0-473-14286-5

EAN-13 9780473142865

Book design and layout by Pipeline Press

Published by Pipeline Press

Preludes

Author:

Jenny Setchell was born in Hunterville, a small country town in the North Island of New Zealand. She received her secondary schooling at Nga Tawa, completed a BA at the University of Otago, and has almost completed a Mus B at the University of Canterbury, majoring in organ performance. Although she has played organs in churches of various denominations for more than 40 years, her principal career has been that of a journalist for most of her working life. In 2005 Jenny left her job as a senior sub-editor at *The Press*, one of New Zealand's main metropolitan daily newspapers, to pursue her freelance activities. These include website design and maintenance, (nzorgan.com) photography (organcalendars.com and organgifts.com), and writing. When time allows and she is not on tour with international concert organist husband Martin, she wrestles with the garden and their two Burmese cats.

Illustrator:

UK-born Terence Dobson studied art at the Watford College of Art. After moving to Australia he gained a BA, and a BEd from the University of Queensland, and an MPhil from Griffith University, Brisbane. He was subsequently awarded his PhD by the University of Canterbury in Christchurch, New Zealand. Apart from illustrating, Terence writes on film animation and recently published a book called *The Film Work of Norman McLaren*, centred on one of the film world's major innovators. He teaches film animation at the University of Canterbury. He has also written on Himalayan film, having often travelled to the Himalayas with his wife, Elaine, a composer and ethnomusicologist.

Cover photograph of Fred Swann: Guy F. Henderson

This book is dedicated
to all those who devote their
hearts and minds, hands and feet
to the service of organ music.

And to

my guardian angels,
David and Althea

Contents

For updates to websites and online links supplied in this volume, and information on how to order more copies, please visit

www.pipeorgan.co.nz

Foreword

Anything with up to 10,000 or so pipes and several miles of wiring and tubing and whatnot is going to be a potential source of problems, and the organ proudly justifies all the fears its players harbour. It sits there, humming quietly to itself (humidifier anyone?) and obviously planning what new surprise to spring on those who approach it with varying degrees of either trepidation or over-confidence. Any time it decides to show pity and behave impeccably for a while, its custodians or passing workmen will more than make up for its quiescence. Perfectly planned rehearsal schedules are merely a challenge to them, as when I checked and re-checked that a certain cathedral organ was available for me to prepare for the first rehearsal of a new concerto that had been commissioned for me to play at the Proms. I arrived with one hour in which to get ready, and heard a piano being tuned. I found the verger and said I was ready to begin; would they please stop the tuner. "Can't do that, I'm afraid!" Through gritted teeth I reminded him that I had confirmed twice in 24 hours that my rehearsal was in the diary. "Oh yes, it is, but so is the piano tuning!" Overcoming my incredulity in favour of essential action, I gained entry to the loft by subterfuge, pulled out every stop and lay down on the keys. End of tuning.

It was no-one's fault that the Swell pedal on the organ for my very first London recital was stiff, but it was a pity that the bench was not anchored more securely. Thrusting the Swell box open in the middle of a virtuosic passage in *Dieu parmi nous* I found myself suddenly back a couple of yards wedged in the music cupboard, my hands still playing the right notes but in the air, my voice pathetically pleading to the page turner "Push me back! Push me back!" Sometimes the organ itself suffers more than anyone; it was tragic that a janitor's pride in his church's new organ led him to polish the front pipes early on the morning of the dedication, with his very best polish. About $30,000 was what it cost to replace those pipes. . .

Arriving at a town hall in the north of England to play another new concerto, to be conducted by the composer and broadcast by the BBC, I was confronted by a phlegmatic city hall employee. "Will you be needing a . . . (he consulted a piece of paper and slowly enunciated the words) Six-teen-foot-fag-ott?" I indicated that I might well be grateful to have use of such a stop. "Well, one of our maintenance men working in the Mayor's office, behind the organ, hammered some nails through and they have gone into the . . . (paper again) six-teen-foot-fag-ott and it won't work".

As a full-time concert organist I encounter different terrors from those dealt with in a church service, and an early struggle with the temporary madness of brides gave me every reason to abandon them. One such bride obediently followed the vicar when he turned to go up to the altar for the second part of the ceremony. On his turning around to face the wedding party again his usual dignity deserted him when he found the bride had vanished. A couple of frantic twirls revealed that she had followed him right into the sanctuary and was now marooned between him and the altar.

Newspaper interviews and the like have their own hazards. One American TV station sent along what must have been their sports reporter or possibly tea boy. An elaborate scene was set up; I was to be discovered dreamily playing Franck, and then he would interview me. I took up my position, and the interviewer, trailing microphone leads, advanced slowly across the scene towards the console, completing his introduction as he reached me with "And now we meet Gillian Weir, one of the world's great organisms!"

Then there are dresses: do wear something non-slippery when playing the Bach D major Prelude and Fugue — it is hard to recover from slipping neatly off the end of the bench after the opening scale. And get there early: when the great Italian organist Fernando Germani's plane was delayed before a concert his subsequent late arrival left him no opportunity for rehearsal. Sportingly, he went out on stage as scheduled and sat down at the organ, but alas, it had not been switched on. He pressed a button, and promptly vanished from sight; the console had sunk without trace. A minute later, the fascinated audience saw him again, as the console rose from the depths and then continued to climb high above them, turning lazily as it went. A moment of contemplation at the summit and a third button was found, and the shaken maestro made a safe landing on terra firma.

Welcome to our world, in the pages within.

Gillian Weir

August 2008

Preface

When asking for anecdotes from organists I specified that the tales did not have to be humorous. The writers — most of whom were organists — were asked to provide a glimpse behind the scenes of their public, performing lives; the incidents or observations could be sad, unusual, amusing, whimsical, or merely diverting. If they bequeathed a humanity to the often invisible figure who makes his or her presence felt Sunday by Sunday in churches around the globe, perfect; if they added a warmer dimension to the remoteness of a two-dimensional character credited on a CD sleeve or music score, wonderful; if they helped to enlighten the non-organist reader, all the better. In short, whatever it took to breathe life into a familiar, but frequently fusty figure, became a welcome offering.

Strictly speaking, anecdote means 'unpublished, private', literally 'not taken out'; it typically refers to a short narrative, usually biographical (readers will recognise many famous names from the music-making world). Other stories have been supplied by a supporting cast of music lovers, onlookers, friends and relatives who have a privileged insight into the organ world, but prefer to keep their identity in the background.

So when reading these pages, look not for the jokes, although many anecdotes will make you smile or even laugh; look, rather, through these windows of words to understand better what it costs these gifted musicians to bring the magical sounds of the organ to our lives.

J.S.

Thanks to. . .

Massimo and Franca Nosetti who, under the beautiful skies of the Italian Alps in Limone Piemonte, finally convinced me to embark on this book, and provided the first story.

More than 600 organ lovers, builders and organists were contacted asking for anecdotes, and nearly 200 replied. To all those musicians and music lovers who took such infinite time and trouble to send me their anecdotes, my deepest thanks; without your stories, let alone your support and encouragement, this book would never have evolved. To those for whom English is not their first language I am especially grateful and hope I have helped massage your words without losing the charm of your original texts. To those who are not in this volume: if you missed out this time, perhaps there will be another. There was simply not enough room for every tale that was worthy of inclusion. Some wished to remain anonymous and will know who they are — thank you nevertheless. In rare cases several people may claim the same, usually apocryphal, anecdote; the provenance of so many stories that circulate in the organ lofts make tracing the original speaker or subjects difficult, so if I have forgotten someone or mis-attributed a quotation, please forgive me.

I am deeply indebted in particular to Christopher Herrick in the UK, Hans Uwe Hielscher in Germany, Fred Swann in the USA, Frank Mento in France and Mark Quarmby and Joy Hearne in Australia, all of whom went beyond the call of duty, either to write stories, or track down the original subjects of stories. The members of the Mander discussion board have kept my quest alive for nearly two years and many informal comments have netted fruitful and joyful stories. Photographer Guy F. Henderson very generously allowed us to reproduce his photograph of Fred Swann and Alicia, the tiger, on the cover.

Thanks to those who put up with my impertinent questions and badgerings for advice and yet more juicy stories. To the indefatigably patient Terence Dobson who translated his own wonderful sense of humour into the illustrations in super-quick time; to Towser Burko and his life-long supportive AIBFF logic; to David and Althea, who were always there to help delve into any kind of problem, contact people, research minutiae and hold my hand over 12,000 miles; to my former journalistic mentor Anton Petre who patiently pruned my randomly peppered commas from the text; to my cargo-ship companion Mary Sketch for her exacting proof-reading expertise; and to our two Burmese cats who thoughtfully added their fur and assorted mice to the computer keyboard as they helped me weave the stories together.

Most of all, heart-felt gratitude to my husband Martin, the best teacher I have ever had, for his endless patience as he endured yet another meal of fish and chips in the course of the birth of this book. Apart from filling my life with glorious music, Martin makes it possible for me to hear so many diverse instruments and meet fellow organists on our journeys around the world.

Jenny Setchell

Christchurch, New Zealand

November, 2008

Acknowledgements and Sources

I am grateful to copyright holders who have freely given permission for use of the material in this book.

Amis, John & Michael Rose. Words About Music. London Wiedenfeld & Nicolson, 1966. (Citing Bowra, see following)

Ampt, Robert. *The Sydney Town Hall Organ — William Hill and Son's Magnum Opus.* 11 the Appian Way, Woodford, Australia: Birralee Publishing, 1999

Bowra, C.M. *Memories 1898-1939.* London : Weidenfeld and Nicolson, 1966 (all attempts to locate a rights holder for the letter were unsuccessful.)

Bunk, Gerard. *Liebe zur Orgel, Erinnerungen aus einem Musikerleben* Dortmund, Germany: Ardey Verlag. 1958 Trans. Hans Hielscher.

Henderson, John. A Directory of Composers for Organ. Swindon, UK.1999. Http://www.rscm.u-net.com

Holmes, Oliver Wendell. *Poems – Songs of many Seasons – In the Quiet Days.* London: G. Routledge & Sons [1886?]

Lindsay, Joyce and Maurice. *The Music Quotation Book.* Copyright ©Joyce & Maurice Lindsey, 1993. First published in Great Britain by Robert Hale Ltd.

Organist's Review, 2004/2 Vol xc No 354, 130-131

Positif Press. *Fanfare for an Organ Builder: Essays presented to Noel Mander to celebrate the 60th anniversary of his commencement in business as an organ-builder.* Oxford, UK: [2005?]

Shaw, Watkins. *A Succession of Organists of the Chapel Royal and the Cathedrals of England and Wales from c.1538 — (Oxford Studies in British Church Music).* Oxford, UK: Clarendon Press, 1991

Venning, Mark. Brochure, Northern Cathedrals Festival, c. [1990?]

Wills, Arthur. *Full with Wills — My Life in My Music: A Memoir.* Brighton, UK: PenPress Publishers, Ltd, 2006.

Websites

- Organ events (UK): www.organrecitals.com
- Organ events (world): www.organfocus.com
- BachOrgan: www.bachorgan.com
- Dame Gillian Weir speech: www.gillianweir.com/articles/birmingham
- Mander Discussion Board:
  www.mander-organs.com/discussion/index.php?
- Pipe Organs and Related Topics: www.albany.edu/piporg-l/
- Encyclopedia of Organ Stops: www.organstops.org
- Organ music on demand: www.organlive.com
- Pipe Dreams: www.pipedreams.org.
- General resources: *archive.org/details/poemshol00holmuoft (Holmes' Poems)*
- General organ resources:
  www.nzorgan.com;
  www.die-orgelseite.de/index_e.html
  www.sydneyorgan.com/Australia.html
  www.rscm.u-net.com

For organists' personal websites, see contributor list beginning page 227

Organists and organs

Manual labour

"Welcome to the world's best-disguised booby trap."

The bride is predictably radiant, the groom similarly luminous; the congregation stands, benign and beaming, and they wait for organist Adrian Taylor to start the wedding recessional.

> "There I am, playing the Charpentier Te Deum (on an organ with a transposing switch), when the pedal department decides that it doesn't like D major. It is now going to play in E major. Up a tone. I struggle through a little bit (I've never tried partial transposition before), but give up with the feet entirely when it pops back down to B flat."

Elsewhere in England, a well-known organist accompanies a Mothers' Union Diocesan service in the Free Trade Hall in Manchester. The Bishop is about to make a grand entrance, so the organist decides to use the snare drum, followed by a big fanfare. The organist unfortunately misjudges his lunge for the snare drum piston and the Bishop makes his grand entrance to "cuckoo — cuckoo — cuckoo".

Welcome to the King of instruments. No, cancel that. Welcome to the world's best-disguised booby trap. And say "Hello folks" to the fraternity of Organists Who Look Silly (O.W.L.S), a grand society of musicians who unwittingly signed up the first day they played an organ in public. Membership is overflowing, by all accounts. No occasion is too great or too small for qualification. Naturally a royal wedding, televised to millions, gains more brownie points for bloopers, ciphers, cock-ups and other entertainments than a small parish Sunday service. To the victim, the hapless, tireless, and perspiring organist, it hurts no less.

A world of difference exists between the concert organist and the church organist. Each has their own set of problems and rewards. A very few organists are both, but most separate the secular from the religious. Professionals differ from non-professionals: those who chose an organ career from childhood, and those who were coerced at the point of a loaded hymn book into transferring their piano-tinkering onto the harmonium for a service once a month. Heart-stopping, side-splitting, and soul-uplifting; unrewarding, thankless, monotonous, exhausting: it's the best and the worst job in the world. So why all the fuss when the organ is really only a piano with wind?

Few people fully understand that the touring concert organist must play his or her programme each time on what amounts to a strange instrument. If they have taken into consideration different audiences, organs and occasions, no two programmes will be identical. Each instrument is unique and has its own robust way of reminding players who is, ultimately, the boss. Nothing is ever in exactly the same place, at the same height, called the same thing, or works the same way.

Imagine the protests if, for instance, a violinist were ordered to play the same programme on a cello with minimal time to learn the thing and with every possible attempt on the part of the global army of vacuum cleaners to sabotage matters. They simply would not do it. Which is why it is so odd that supposedly sane organists undertake tours.

In an ideal world, for every 10 minutes of performance time an organist will generally need one hour of preparation. The rehearsal is not primarily about practising the notes, or brushing up on technique — that must be assumed as already in top-notch condition; it is a time for the organist to get to know whatever contraption they are faced with, and to orchestrate the sounds on that particular instrument, in that building, in that acoustic. The organist chooses what sound to use for every note of the music; it must be balanced so that the sound of the pedals does not obscure that of the manuals, the voices in contrapuntal works all speak with clarity, and the music makes a harmonious whole. This is often referred to as choosing the registration, or registering. With roughly 360 distinctly different stop types to work with (and around 2200 if you add the name variations [1]) that is a lot of decision-making. Even other keyboard players, such as pianists, have it easy by comparison. A pianist works solely with the sound and touch of the piano, and that is it. The organist must spend time (sometimes a long time in difficult acoustics and with awkward instruments) selecting how to paint his music with the colours of the organ. Organists have twice the number of appendages to worry about as well: an organist is to a pianist what an octopus is to a limpet — all limbs are go, with the feet as important as the hands.

So when the organ died completely only minutes before a concert in Great Malvern Priory, the bright spark who suggested that Martin Setchell should simply shift his concert and audience to a little country church to perform the programme there an hour or two later, needed his head testing. It just does not work like that. But a pianist could have easily changed venues and instruments at short notice.

Organs do have many stop names in common, so you will find Diapason, Trumpet, Celeste, Mixture, Flute and so on crop-

1 Stauff. *Encyclopedia of Organ Stops*, www.organstops.org

ping up from Oamaru to Oslo. But one organ's mellow moo is another's raucous screech, and it is impossible to judge the sound by name alone. Playing aids, both mechanical and electronic, have endless variations of ingenious systems that allow a player to preselect groups of stops. The catch is that what someone else has set may not (indeed, probably will not) suit the next person. Using preset pistons blindly is one way to get an adrenaline rush that leaves a vertical roller coaster for dead.

Once the sound combinations have been selected, the organist plays the programme to check the "orchestration". If the stops are to be hand-drawn, finding the stop knobs and pistons in a microsecond has to be rehearsed (and ideally with help from the dubiously termed 'assistant' as well) because the layout of a console is never quite the same from one organ to another. Even if there is a sequencer or a stepper (a digital system that captures the stops the player has selected and will call back the registration at the appropriate points — in theory) it needs to be tested to ensure that the set combinations work as they should.

The console of a large three to five manual organ is closer to the design of an Airbus 380 cockpit than a keyboard. Just as for pilots, it behoves the organist to know what all the little lights mean, especially the tempting red one that says 'Do Not Press'. (It is said that before the organ in Truro was worked on by Willis in the 1960s, a system of indicator lights on the console warned "Bride at West Door" and so on, and one of the lights was the signal for "You're playing the wrong tune".) For a bonus challenge, 'authentic' historic organs may bear scrawled Gothic lettering on the stop knobs that needs translating and memorising. Added piquancy comes with mechanical and electrical woes such as pipes ciphering (where a note keeps sounding), stops jamming and wind supply not working. If a page turner or stop-changer is helping, it is a good idea to rehearse with them beforehand, as well.

At the highly visible organ in Christchurch Town Hall, a visiting organist forgot to tell me as page turner that some pages of his score were manuscript, with large chunks of music crossed out.

This made judging where his flying fingers were in relation to the score a little tricky, and an emergency Grunt-and-Nod method had to suffice. Consider too, the organist who forgot to warn her helper that she had removed several pages from a loose-leaf set of 12 Variations on a Theme. The sudden jump between page numberings had an ashen-faced page turner scrabbling through the dog-eared pages at the console, convinced she was responsible for miscounting.

Even resident organists who have grown to know and love the monster they drive almost every day are nervously aware that the beast can, unprovoked, throw a tantrum by refusing to speak. Instead, it may refuse to stop speaking — either way it threatens heart failure. This is timed, like all good tantrums, to coincide with the visit of a bishop, or during spectacular Easter services rehearsed for weeks as the highlight of the church musical year. Is it so surprising that organists get a little tetchy when those precious minutes of rehearsal are stolen from them?

Organist groupies (of which I count myself a faithful member) have even more reason to be at least grey, if not completely bald. We watch in horror as the bag lady rustles up the aisle to seat herself as close as possible to the organist where she can play a continuo with her packaging. We are the enterprising helpers who must find the loft keys which some priest is rumoured to keep, but his location, name, and the Polish/German/French/Korean word for key are all unknown. We are the companions at the end of the night when everyone else has gone home, and the only sounds are the water dripping into a bucket under the leaking roof, and the wind moaning under the door at the west end.

This is only the beginning of the fun...

Giving concerts

Rehearsing, or, the battle of the vacuum cleaners

"The Judge says, if you don't shut up he'll have you for contempt of Court."

The concert organist's world is encumbered by well-meaning helpers, moving parts, non-moving parts, guided tour groups, locks, electricity, clergy, and vacuum cleaners. All-important rehearsal time is when a player is most likely to encounter these hurdles. The greatest performers are not exempt. Consider those at the very top, as Alan Morrison did, when he hosted Gillian Weir in Philadelphia. The first hitch was a change in venue caused by renovations at the original location.

Alan outlined the situation to Gillian, explaining that since it was not his venue he had no control over conditions, but had asked that her practice time be, naturally enough, quiet and uninterrupted.

> "As we walked in she said she was used to interruptions (as we all are when on the road) and that Catherine Crozier had long ago told her on one of her first trips to

> the USA, 'Now Gillian, everyone knows that here in the USA every organ blower is connected to a vacuum cleaner.' At which point I opened the doors to the sanctuary to let her enter . . . and a vacuum cleaner went on. She threw her hands up in the air in a dramatic gesture and said, 'SEE?'"

The predatory vacuum cleaner is a global pest and stalks victims in every country that has organs. David Aprahamian Liddle, weary from battle, suggested someone should write a *Suck and blow* concerto for the hundreds of hoovers that whined in counterpoint as he tried to rehearse in the Royal Albert Hall.

In the USA, Joan DeVee Dixon went as far as devising a title for one of her compositions as *Hoover in F*, and Emma Lou Diemer suggested that Joan compose a trio for 32ft Contra-Bombarde, Hoover and Leaf Blower. The piece has yet to be performed as the women cannot decide if custodial staff should be invited to play their instruments as soloists. (A shame. It would be a gift for a two-word concert review: "*It sucks*"). Joan's catalogue of general annoyances typifies the problems organists face.

> "Some custodians decide to work only after I arrive. After all, many people enjoy listening to music as they work. It is also true that some do this just to be annoying (many consider it is their duty to drive you out). In Huntsville I somehow managed to practise Liszt's *Liebestraum* (in A flat) while the sound booth was playing '*This is My Father's World*' in the key of G, and the custodian was vacuuming in the key of A. There have been times when the organ tutti has come in handy.
>
> It seems that in my travels, I have encountered an over-abundance of other distractions. In Oxford, staff were tearing down tables and dropping them on the floor. Periodic cymbal crashes in my left ear would have had a less dramatic effect. In Iowa, a piano student began practising diligently downstairs while I was play-

ing the organ upstairs. In the Ozarks, a wedding party came into the chapel and started nailing things to the walls. I finally had to call for help.

In Switzerland, one video monitor included a TV with Mass, CNN, and the World Cup. As if none of this was bad enough, I have performed concerts during a 17-year plague of cicadas on an organ console laden with lady bugs (church people kept telling me 'Don't squish the bugs'), and in temperatures ranging from 50 to over 100 degrees."

All organists have discovered that their carefully scheduled rehearsals have conflicted with events not listed on the church calendar, or even concert hall schedule. Joan has forfeited practice time for bus tours, a First Grade Rosary, Santa Claus, stage construction (and demolition), and sound system installations, complete with testing. At a church in Minneapolis, the staff energetically removed the church's 30-foot Christmas trees with chainsaws. The church was full of smoke when the organ tuners arrived. The chaplain reassured Joan that the deafening fire alarm would last only three hours.

"After this episode, I gave up all hope of ever having a quiet place to practise. Thus, when it was suggested in Tennessee that I play the grand piano in the gym while the softball girls were practising their off-season pitching, I figured, 'What have I got to lose?' Aside from the few stray balls that zinged past my head, it was the most pleasant group that I have ever accompanied. Who would have thought?"

Arthur Wills[2] wrote of the time he arrived early in Vancouver, Canada, anxious to set up and rehearse before the inaugural concert on the newly rebuilt organ, but was instead taken on a suspiciously long tour of the city. When Arthur finally arrived at the church, he discovered the reason for the delaying tactics. The organ

2 Wills: *Full with Wills - My Life in My Music: A Memoir. 209*

was still being, well, organised, as the innards strewn over the floor demonstrated. After a bit of pressure from Arthur, the organ was playable by the morning of the concert two days later — but the piston mechanism refused to work. It would have to be hand-drawn stops, at least 50 of them. After the resident organist made an introduction and explained the difficulties arising, Arthur recounted the story of Walter Parratt (organist of St George's Chapel, Windsor) who "was frequently asked to open organs, but was heard to say that very many times he would prefer to close them."

Cloddish offenders are often disarmingly unaware of problems their noise might cause — after all, they can still do their work with the organ playing at the same time, can't they? Arriving to practise at a venue in Arizona, Martin Setchell found the auditorium seating being removed for a refit. Chirpy workmen with jackhammers were not bothered by his arrival at all: "You play away; it doesn't worry us". Martin resigned himself to the inevitable cacophony.

> "To make matters worse, they got every seat back in time for the concert — just — thus denying me the opportunity to claim a standing ovation in the States."

When James Welch was a graduate student at Stanford he was rehearsing the Charles Ives *Variations on America* over and over on the Hradtezky organ in the concert hall on campus. At the same time a construction worker was breaking up concrete to repair some seating in the hall.

> "The noise from the sledgehammer was driving me crazy, but I had a recital coming up, so I continued practising. After some time I paused my practice, and the workman said, 'Hey, kid, could you take a cigarette break for a while? That music is driving me crazy'!"

You never know who you will meet during rehearsals. Martin and I had been locked in alone — or so we thought — at St Paul's Cathedral in London to register for his concert the next day. I was walking about, listening in the dimming shadows, when I turned a corner and bumped straight into man who came out of the darkness. Suppressing a scream, I could not for the life of me remember who he was, but recognised his face and assumed he was someone I knew from back home in New Zealand. I gibbered away happily. "Hello! What are YOU doing here?" Wild eyed, he muttered something and fled, leaving me to puzzle over where I had seen him before. Only when I saw a BBC camera crew setting up to film an historic drama at a side door of the cathedral (complete with tinkling props, shouted directions, and other filming accompaniments) did the truth dawn. It was the famous actor Hugh Laurie.

Rehearsal, for the perfectionist, extends far beyond simply playing the notes. Karl Richter was master of theatrical presentations. When John Mander was working for organ builders von Beckerath, a couple of his colleagues were working on the organ in the Musikhalle in Hamburg in preparation for a concert by Richter.

> "They heard a door slam followed by purposeful footsteps across the stage and a thump as somebody sat at the console. When this happened a couple of times more they investigated and discovered Karl Richter practising his entrance for the evening recital."

Richter's preparation for a recital at the Royal Festival Hall mystified Ralph Downes, who was listening outside the auditorium. He heard Richter play the last bar of the fugue in D (BWV 532). Diddle-iddle dum, DUM DUM. After a few seconds, there it was again: Diddle-iddle dum, DUM DUM. After 10 minutes of this, Downes went in to see what was happening. Richter was practising pushing himself off the stool with the last pedal note, spinning round as he did so, to land on the floor behind the organ console, then taking a bow — all in one swift movement.

Wise performers will even rehearse their entrances because some venues have such a labyrinth of doors, stairs and passages that finding the way on stage is a challenge. One player at the

Christchurch Town Hall made a less than glorious approach through the startled audience in the balcony stalls.

Some performers truly do risk serious consequences for devotion to their art. Roy Massey's attempts to get in some practice resulted in a swift brush with the law.

> "It used to be a fact that many of the Town Halls in England often shared their premises with the local Law Courts. One day I was practising in the Victoria Hall, Hanley, for a recital as part of an IAO Conference. The organ in those days was in a pretty bad way and my rehearsal time was constantly interrupted with things going wrong. Fortunately the local tuner was with me but my practice time was slipping by with little being achieved.
>
> This was worrying, as the audience would be an informed one, largely made up of organists, and naturally I was keen to do my best. Therefore I carried on practising after lunch until a little man appeared and asked me to stop. By this time I was getting impatient so I told him quite brusquely that I had a concert that evening and really must do some work in preparation for it. He went away, only to re-appear 10 minutes later with the message: 'the Judge says, if you don't shut up he'll have you for contempt of Court.'
>
> I stopped."

Locked in

"We were both woken by an eerie clang of the cathedral bell. I sat up in bed and suddenly remembered my organ student."

People who run large public buildings have a fondness for locks and keys, and the two do not always connect happily. Key custodians are suspicious of strange musical types who arrive to play the organ. They like to lock them up rather than let them loose in their building, preferably at night, out of sight, and definitely out of hearing. The very idea of giving organists a key and/or clear instructions as to how to get out of the building is anathema. Cellphones have latterly saved incarcerated organists from dining off the pages of *Hymns Ancient and Modern* for survival, but they have also removed the potential for the character-building challenges that the older school of organists had to tackle.

Even Massimo Nosetti, with his finely-honed skills adapted to the vagaries of organs and their housing, fell foul of the Lock in an Organist brigade. After an afternoon practising in a pleasant little Italian concert hall he collected his belongings, turned off the instrument, pulled the main door of the hall to lock automatically behind him, and reached the exit door (the only one in the building that led to the street). The concierge, who had already left, had assured him that nobody would have entered the hall or locked the door. Naturally, Massimo found this last door locked, and he had no key.

Massimo realised that because it was late in the afternoon on a Saturday, he was stuck there until Monday morning. The only public phone in the hall was on the second floor, access to which he had also locked behind him. It was not looking good. He was faced with staying for a couple of days and nights in the lobby with no water, no food, and no toilet (it was also on the second floor). Even by yelling through the thick main door which led to a small side street he still could not be heard. After a couple of hours spent thinking about life, the universe, and his unusual predicament, Massimo decided it was time he became a burglar — but one who needed to get out, rather than in.

> "I took a chair in order to reach the single, very narrow window in the lobby, and I broke the glass with my briefcase and wriggled through the little window into the nearby courtyard of a private house. Then I found an open door leading into the kitchen and, from there, I walked to the main door of the house in the dark, fortunately with no alarms, and so to the outside. If somebody had discovered me there in the middle of the night, even quite elegantly dressed and with a briefcase full of organ scores, it would have been quite difficult, and surely embarrassing, to explain what I was up to."

Lord Aylesford was privy to an incident during the Second World War. Two American GIs, stationed in England, obtained permission to play the 1749 organ in Packington church, Warwickshire. The person responsible for locking up failed to check that the building was empty; hence they found themselves held firmly behind stout doors. Due back at base and anxious to attract attention to their plight, they made as much noise as possible with the church bell. Unknown to them, the ringing of church bells was reserved as a signal that an invasion had taken place and there was an absolute embargo on their use for any other purpose. When the doors were finally unlocked, the soldiers found an interested group of senior people from the army, ARP, Home Guard and other organisations anxious to learn exactly where the enemy were to be found.

When David Rumsey arrived in Basel he was asked to go on a list of supplementary organists who played at the local necropolis. Just before Christmas he agreed to play for an urgent funeral, then learned that the requested repertoire included the Bach Fantasia and Fugue in G minor at the beginning and end respectively. David gulped, and said he would have to practise in the chapel that afternoon.

> "I arrived there as darkness fell, and began practising. A tremendous storm with wind and sleet began during my first hour there, the chapel dimmed, and spooks knocked on the windows (branches) or howled in the ceiling (wind). After a couple of hours I had done what I could and started to leave, only to discover that the whole necropolis had long since shut down, was in total darkness except for pallid icy tombstones and dark, unlit wind-blown paths. I was alone and locked in with an uncertain chance of getting out that night.
>
> I stumbled and slid towards the main gate, through 300 metres or so of graves that all seemed to be moving as the trees danced a macabre frenzy in the gale. Fortunately, however, it was Christmas and a huge tree had been erected outside the gate. Its blinking lights were a distant beacon and at least showed me the way to freedom. I found an old gnarled vine on the inside and somehow clambered up it — the great gates of doom here are at least three metres high — and across a solid stone pillar, into the upper branches of an illuminated Christmas tree which must have been at least four metres tall.

> You can imagine the looks on the faces of people waiting opposite the gate at the bus stop when this apparition, hair standing on end, emerged from the pitch-black graveyard, scuttled to the top of the tree, threw a briefcase on the ground, followed it with a mighty thump, branches and decorative lights trailing in its wake. There was nothing I could do but join the bus queue and ride with them, the focus of many an odd glance as all moved to other parts of the vehicle and left me well alone."

David Aprahamian Liddle's experience with technology has been dogged by bad luck. Locked inside Westminster Cathedral in London for the first of two long evening rehearsals, David, who is blind, and a sighted friend had been given an electronic key to let them out of the door that connects the cathedral to Clergy House. But by the time he had finished and was bracing himself for the underground night-time journey home, the door, which had a reputation for being awkward, would not open.

> "We tried the electronic key every way, becoming ever more frantic. In despair, we turned to a telephone, with a long list of extensions beside it. We sighed with relief as we noticed the first number given was for reception in Clergy House. After ringing this number for ages, we concluded that reception had gone to bed long since. We considered phoning Cardinal Basil Hulme, but eventually tried the Sisters of Mercy. A sleepy nun who answered the phone took a while to understand the situation; at first, she urged us to sleep on a bed in the Choir School, but she finally realised our predicament. She nobly got up, dressed, crossed the road and roused a resident of Clergy House, who eventually rescued us. This has happened to me with the electronic keys at Westminster Cathedral more than once."

Imprisoned inside Chester Cathedral for a long evening practice with a sighted friend, David was given a two-way radio so they could alert their host when they were ready to leave.

> "Exhausted and ready to collapse after hours of concentration, I tried the radio at 11pm, but discovered there was no signal. I had visions of sleeping on a stone tomb, but luckily, after half an hour or so, our host came to check that all was well."

Cathedrals such as Chester are well-known as forts from which escape is impossible for practising recitalists and their helpers. One abandoned soul, however, had the presence of mind to use the console phone (an otherwise pointless tool unless there is a nearby list of emergency phone numbers) to call the police for help.

Unlike many ancient church buildings in the United Kingdom and Europe, Chester Cathedral does have a toilet inside, but it is inside the vestry, which is locked unless you have the foresight to ask before being left to practise. Try not to have a stomach bug at the time. . .

One of the more aurally unpleasant experiences (apart from a massive cipher) is an alarm going off close by. What if you cannot disarm it or get out of its range? Christopher Herrick was preparing for his concert in a Danish church, the exit door of which was behind the altar, invisible from the body of the building. He had been told to set the burglar alarm when he had finished practising, and was assured that the door would open easily from inside and self-lock on closing.

> "After finishing my preparation all I had to do was punch a code into the alarm system and leave by that door. Unfortunately, having set the alarm, imagine my dismay when, going behind the altar I found the solid door in question wide open but another slatted door firmly locked in its place. The caretaker had done this to 'air' the building. My continued presence naturally set an ear-piercing alarm going, and it was the best part of half

> an hour before anyone came to rescue me. On my release, I was a nervous wreck."

From experience, Christopher says it is also vital to know where the toilet facilities are when locked in a building for a prolonged period of concert preparation.

> "A small Polish cathedral near the Russian border was the scene of one of my more surreal experiences. I was met by an old professorial type and a young lad when I got off the rickety bus, which had been pounding over the rather uneven roads from Gdansk for a full eight hours. As my Polish and Russian are non-existent and their German and French ditto, we had to rely on the boy's extremely slender grasp of English to establish communication. They installed me at the organ with a promise that a nun would let me out of the building at a certain hour.
>
> Luckily, I remembered to enquire after the toilet — a fairly international word. They took me there before leaving, and I decided to make use of the facility there and then. It was a partitioned area inside the building and the loo-seat was held in an upright position in an improvised manner by a broom handle. My business completed, I went to open the door only to find it had no handle inside and I was therefore effectively locked in. This was a good start to the proceedings. Removing the broom handle and lowering the loo seat, I stood up on it and called loudly over the partition, 'Hallo! Zu Hilfe!'
>
> Thank goodness I was answered by the shuffling feet of an old lady who was still putting things away. She let me out, demonstrating in a dumb show how I should have taken the handle off the outside of the door and then placed it on the inside to facilitate getting out. Silly me! Why didn't I think of that?"

One winter evening David Willcocks was giving a young man an organ lesson when he remembered an urgent phone call that he needed to make.

> "I left the student practising while I ran home across the Close. At that time, Salisbury Cathedral was closed at dusk, so I locked the door as I left. After making the telephone call, I had supper with Rachel and we went to bed. In the middle of the night, we were both woken by an eerie clang of the cathedral bell. I sat up in bed and suddenly remembered my organ student. I raced across the Close in my pyjamas and dressing-gown, and unlocked the cathedral. The nave was in utter darkness except for a small light up in the organ loft. My student, realising that he had been abandoned, had played the organ with all the stops out, trying in vain to alert me. Then he had groped his way through the pitch dark nave to the west end, where he had found a bell rope. What I remember most is that he apologised profusely for waking me, and had only done so because he knew his widowed mother would be worried."

Another night-time victim was Gerard Brooks:

"Playing a recital in Trier, Germany, I had to practise at night, and the church was very dark. I felt my way up to the organ loft and then searched for a light switch. I tried several possible switches without success; after a while I began to wonder why the bells were ringing so late at night . . . until I realised I had switched on the automatic carillon."

Locked out

" ... the organist had left town, taking with him what they believed was the only key to the large Gonzalez"

Getting access to an organ should be an entrance exam for burglars; often it is the organist with the finest lock-picking skills who gets to practise the longest. Over the last 30 years giving recitals, Paul Derrett reckons he has coped with at least 12 fraught occasions when nobody has been at the venue to greet him or let him in.

> "I have arrived to find power cables sawn through, pistons that have stuck on, notes that have ciphered, officials who have said caustic rather than apologetic things despite arriving hours late to let us in. Most times I have a minder and virtually every time we have got by. Even so, quite a few times I have come away from a lunchtime recital vowing never to do it again."
>
> At least three of these concerts were done without any rehearsal whatsoever. In one spectacular case, the recital was not even given on the organ it was intended for, but in St Clement Danes down the road, where church officials had taken pity on me and my audience."

Across the channel in France, Paul found matters to be, if anything, worse. Twenty or so years ago he went to give a recital in Rheims Cathedral. When he arrived to rehearse at 10 am for the lunchtime concert he was told the organist had left town, taking with him what they believed was the only key to the large Gonzalez.

> "As time ticked away, searches for a spare key (if they were ever in earnest, which is a good question in itself) proved fruitless. About ten minutes before the published start time (and remember these things can be very flexible indeed in France) someone offered me the key to the Choir organ. This was quite a worrying prospect, since its case (around 20 feet tall) both above and behind the player, leaned into the cathedral at an angle of 85 degrees. Not holding out my hopes for much, I was not surprised when the first note I played (bottom C on the pedals) went down and stayed down. I think the rest of the programme ended up being for manuals only."

Playing in an historic church in Switzerland, Hans Hielscher was given a huge bone-like key to the gallery that housed the organ. He prepared his programme for the evening, then locked the door behind him to take a break before the concert. He returned at 8 pm, but instead of going to the gallery, he was taken by the vicar to the nave so he could tell the audience about his programme.

> "Having done this, I walked up to the organ gallery. But I was unable to unlock the gallery door with the shapeless big key. It just didn't work. I tried to turn it gently, then violently, I drew it backwards and forwards, turned it in all directions. Nothing happened.
>
> After nearly 10 minutes, I thought of my audience, impatiently waiting for me to begin my Bach prelude. I already could hear a certain, rising murmuring and chatting from the nave — where the heck has the organist gone? I am sure they must have heard these strange

noises from the gallery door (hopefully not my curses). Finally, after I had paused for a while, I tried it a last time, and it worked immediately.

The moral of the story is, do not do anything in a rush, especially not as a soloist before an organ recital. Instead, calm down, relax and you can do anything successfully — even turn a key in its hole."

Hans did not have much luck with an antipodean alarm system either. No surprise there, since itinerant organists consider alarm systems as one of the top ten horrors they meet on the road. But Hans now wonders why some churches have them at all. He had been instructed how to switch off the alarm temporarily at St Andrew's Cathedral in Sydney, Australia, when leaving after practice late at night. Simple stuff. Easy as cracking your ankles against a choir pew in the dark.

"In a pale light, coming from outside, I eventually found the small alarm board and tapped my four digits, and then OK. An ear-splitting siren howled outside. I was so startled that I tried re-entering the code several times, looking for an OFF button. No way, and that awful sound continued. After about five minutes, I thought: 'OK, the police will be here in a minute, what do I tell them? A stranger, with a foreign accent, at midnight in the cathedral, with a suspicious handbag?' Nothing happened and 10 minutes passed. But the siren screamed on.

Eventually I decided to leave the church and locked the door from outside. I had expected crowds waiting to grab and hold me before the police arrived. But to my astonishment no one was standing outside next to that door with the ever-sounding siren. All this, despite St Andrew's Cathedral being in the centre of the city, next to the town hall.

It seemed that this siren, although loud inside, was just one of many other noises around the church. I was somewhat relieved when I got safely to my hotel; but I could still hear that siren, that nobody cared about."

No feathers were ruffled either when a siren suddenly screamed of its own accord in St Giles Cathedral, Scotland, while Martin and I were incarcerated for an evening practice session. Since it was on the eve of a visit by the Queen, we steeled ourselves for a personal visit by the police, army, SIS, MI5 and possibly the navy. But after 15 minutes, no-one had arrived to throw us in the tower, and the alarm mercifully stopped. We continued blissfully as before.

In concert

"It was just a shame that he had forgotten to draw any stops."

Having battled vacuum cleaners, locked doors, ciphers, and sulking organs, the well-prepared organist should find performance if not exactly a breeze, at least the satisfying culmination of hours of preparation. But things can go horribly, and from the audience point of view, deliciously wrong.

As Robert Ampt puts it, when the 'moment of glory eventually arrives' for an organ entry when playing with an orchestra, it really is quite something. He should know: Rob frequently arranges organ parts for works to be played on the Sydney Town Hall Hill organ, of which he has been the organist for 30 years. On one occasion, Tchaikovsky's *1812 Overture* with Rob's organ part added was being performed with the combined Royal Australian Naval Fleet Band and Royal Australian Naval Support Command Band (Sydney). Rob took the precaution of following the music with a miniature score because the organ entry was well into the piece (he was asked later by several sharp-eyed souls what book he had been reading). But at least he was ready for his entry and the moment of great glory for the organ. It was just a shame that he had forgotten to draw any stops.

Humans, particularly those anxious to help, can be relied upon to throw figurative spanners into the organ works. John

Longhurst had a momentary excursion into Hell during a doctoral recital at the Eastman School of Music's Kilbourn Hall. During the intermission he had asked a fellow student to alter one of his previously set pistons by adding the 32ft bombarde stop to the pedal stops in the existing registration, to be used in the toccata from Duruflé's *Suite,* Op. 5.

> "When I reached that climactic moment in the piece and pressed the piston, to my horror the *only* stop set on the piston was the 32ft bombarde — nothing else in the Pedal, and nothing in the manuals. Now as any organist will attest, the Bombarde is hardly what you could call a subtle sonority. In fact, in its lower register it sounds something akin to a machine gun that has had a couple of music lessons. There it was, for all to hear in all its splendour. So I kicked on the crescendo pedal as quickly as I could and ploughed my way through to the end, completely unnerved and chagrined by the experience."

The weather also plays its part in contriving to upset the best-laid plans. In the 1950s, the Westminster Choral Society gave an annual series of performances in Westminster City Hall: Messiah at Christmas, a Passion at Easter and two or three other works during the course of the year. These were accompanied on the organ by George Thalben-Ball; the conductor was Alan Brown, another well-known London organist of the day. The main hall was laid out in conventional manner with the organ at the back, and the choir seated on a stage in front. On December 6, 1952, the late Robin James and David Bridgeman-Sutton made one of their regular visits to hear Messiah. David describes the scene of what was to be the last — and worst — of the great London smogs; Clean Air Acts produced rapid improvement.

> "The weather had been foggy for some days and was getting worse when we arrived. Despite central heating, the hall was decidedly misty. Outside, buses were moving at walking pace, led by the conductors carrying torches; cab-drivers, who proverbially know London like

the backs of their hands, were stopping pedestrians whom they had narrowly avoided knocking down, to ask if any knew where Westminster Bridge had gone, and only faint glimmers revealed the whereabouts of street lighting. Underground and train services, though disrupted, continued and afterwards we got home without too much delay.

During the evening, the fog thickened even inside the hall, lifting during choruses (warm air rising?) and rapidly descending during solos. Toward the end of part two, it was thick enough completely to blanket the organ and back rows of the chorus,which became invisible from the auditorium when the chorus was silent. Despite this handicap, the performance was completed; a casualty was the trumpet soloist who, apparently affected by the smog, produced curious and un-Handelian sounds in the obbligato to *The Trumpet Shall Sound*.

Later, I asked Alan Brown — from whom I was then having lessons — how he and Thalben-Ball remained in touch when visibility was at its worst. 'Telepathy, dear boy', he replied."

Like any past organ scholar at King's College Chapel, John Wells is familiar with the organ there, so fronting up to play Buxtehude's *Prelude in G minor* was going to be simple. He rehearsed, registered, had no problems, and was 100 per cent confident. It was an old favourite piece, old favourite organ. So what could possibly go wrong?

"Off we go. Get to the thundering pedal entry: nothing, zippo, no pedal stops out! Notwithstanding all the advice I give to students, it was such a catastrophe (and at the beginning of a concert, too) that I stopped; it was so unexpected, it completely threw me. In emergencies, preferably *without* stopping, a quick look at the stops should immediately tell you what you have overlooked.

> This time, I looked — and looked — and still couldn't see the problem."

The pedal stops were certainly in when they should not have been, but Gt to Ped. combs stop was out. John pressed Gt whatever it was, but still no pedal stops. It might have been a malfunction — yes, very, very rare at King's, but it has been known. John's brain then fevered into overdrive.

> "I was resigned to make do, and then, through the rising mists of panic, I saw it. Gt to Ped. combs was not out after all, it was Ped. to Gt combs. I mean, dyslexic or what? I had never, ever come across that stop, save at King's, and it was so long ago that it never occurred to me that such a stop even existed. Overconfidence bred carelessness, and I had indeed goofed. Funnily enough, a very short while later I came across the very same set-up on the Harrison at Temple Church in London. Ready for it that time!"

Then there are moments when an organist wonders if they deserve what Fate, or more precisely, what some fellow organist, has done to them. Katherine Dienes-Williams arrived at Liverpool Anglican Cathedral the night she was to perform the Poulenc Organ Concerto with the Royal Liverpool Philharmonic Orchestra. On checking her pre-set generals, she found that all of them had been altered; recovering from the shock, she had the time to reset them, as well as reset her palpitating heart.

Richard Elliott was not quite so fortunate. As one of the main organists for the Mormon Tabernacle Choir in Salt Lake City, Utah, he knows the value of careful and thorough preparation, and just how easily it can still go wrong. By far Richard's most humbling experience of this as a professional organist came during a concert in 2003 inauguration of the new 130-rank, five-manual Schoenstein organ in the Conference Center of the Church of Jesus Christ of Latter-day Saints. Around 16,000 of the 21,000 seats were filled with listeners, a good number of whom either had a hand in the building of the organ or who were attending a multi-region convention of the American Guild of Organists. One of the pieces on the programme was Leonard Bernstein's challenging *Chichester Psalms*, which was being performed in an adaptation for choir, organ, and a small instrumental ensemble.

"I had run through everything the night before and felt confident that I had everything under control. As soon as I played the first chord, I realised something was wrong. The registrations I had carefully worked out were not where they were supposed to be. Was something wrong with the instrument? I verified that I was on the correct memory level and the correct piston, but instead of strong principal and reed choruses I was getting slushy strings. The President of Schoenstein & Co, Jack Bethards, was seated a few rows back and knew right away something was amiss when he saw me looking back and forth between the displays and the controls in the drawer under the left stop jamb, but he also knew that it was not a time for him to intervene.

While a few of my pistons were discovered to be intact, I had to hand register nearly everything on the fly, using the crescendo pedal liberally in order to provide adequate support for the choir. It is a tall order under any circumstance, but to have to do so under the pressure of an organ inauguration *and* an organists' convention *and* a crowd of 16,000 results in an unusually high degree of stress. Somehow we all made it to the final cadence and few people seemed the wiser.

An ensuing investigation revealed that a participant in a master class on the day of the concert had not realised that memory levels were assigned and had set her pistons on the memory level (my memory level) that popped up when she turned the organ on. In the weeks and months that followed, I repeated in my mind over and over the maxim: 'To err is human; to forgive is divine'."

Experienced organists will vouch that when you find yourself performing a Hades version of aural custard, the best thing to do is to bluff your way out. It very often works. Here is bluffery in action. In the 1970s Martin Setchell was playing organ continuo for the annual Messiah performance in the Christchurch Town Hall, using a small chamber organ. Part one went smoothly as expected, and after a short interval, the players reassembled on stage for the second part. It was only as the conductor entered that Martin realised the organ motor had been switched off at the mains offstage during the interval by helpful hands unseen. He was firmly wedged in the midst of the players and could not leave the stage. Frantic semaphore and eye rolling at dark figures in the wings only further convinced onlookers that musicians are not to be trusted unless fully dosed with whatever pills they should be on.

The conductor began, unaware anything was amiss. Martin was literally and figuratively powerless to do anything so he chose the bluffery method of survival. There, centre-stage and in full view of the audience, he meticulously pulled stops, turned pages, and played the notes as a man fired with a mission — without making a sound. After the concert the conductor embraced him with his usual bonhomie.

"Gee Martin, that was great!" drooled the conductor.
"I thought you played even better in the second half."

Bluffing is nothing new. Samuel Sebastian Wesley at Hereford is reported to have made a hash of accompanying the anthem, so he asked his assistant to play the final voluntary. He then left the organ loft, appearing outside the cathedral to greet worshippers to give the appearance that he had not been responsible for the music that day.

Excessive heat or cold is a common problem for performers. Ecclesiastical buildings are excellent training grounds for polar explorers. Christopher Herrick recorded Liszt's and Mendelssohn's works for the BBC in Merseburg Cathedral in former East Germany in sub-zero temperatures, with only a little stove between him and the Rückpositiv (the division of the organ placed at the organist's back, in front of the gallery). But experiences at the other extreme are equally possible.

> "Perhaps after years of acclimatisation my body has learnt to cope with the cold; when the temperature is at a higher level, I tend to become uncomfortable. One summer in Denmark the temperature stayed consistently high for weeks. The effect was tropical, particularly as the heat tended to rise from already over-hot churches and got trapped in the confined space of the organ loft. Having under-performed at one of my concerts because of the excessive heat, I became a bit militant. For the next concert, given in a glass-sided church, I remained in my normal outdoor summer wear with a light-weight, short-sleeved shirt and trousers. I explained and apologised for my lack of formal concert gear to the audience, but little did they guess that once I was safely out of view behind the Rückpositiv, I then also discarded my shirt. Is this the first topless organ concert?"

Hellish seconds can develop into nightmarish eternities. One of my favourite horror stories may be some consolation for others experiencing their own mortifying moments. It is an extraordinary, but alas, true tale, involving a pianist, an organist, a Governor-General, and a Maori concert party.

The opening of the Christchurch Teachers' College auditorium required one fully escorted, formally-robed Governor General of New Zealand, in this case Sir Keith Holyoake, former Prime Minister. In addition was a full entourage, with minders, clatterings of press photographers, and a zillion underlings. A specialist school choir was formed and trained by Frank, the music department head. Frank was to accompany on piano, and Russell Kent would play the organ; Russell's teacher was even there to witness the star pupil at work. The ceremony programme included three main musical items: first, everyone singing the National anthem *God Defend New Zealand;* second, the choir performing Bach's *Nun Danket;* and finally, massed singing of *God Save the Queen.* Easy as falling off an organ bench. There was not the slightest sign of trouble. Russell carefully spread his music neatly on the music desk, Frank put his scores on the grand piano and they both waited.

The vice-regal party cruised into position, so Russell and Frank launched into the National Anthem. At least, Russell did. Frank, for reasons best known to himself, put his head down and crashed into *God Save the Queen.* Half the audience sided with Russell and the other half had their sympathies with Frank. Russell was appalled but, armed with the louder weapon, stuck grimly to *God Defend New Zealand.* On the opposing team, Frank was busily saving the Queen. Both halves of the audience initially bellowed their own supporting verses, aided by the choir, which was evenly divided, until after several minutes the entire bawling session subsided to an embarrassed mix of giggles and grunts. Frank, realising at last what he had done, slunk off the piano stool and into a corner.

The Maori concert party gathered on stage to welcome the vice-regal entourage, so like it or not, Russell had to move from the console to make room for the performers as they crowded around the organ. After a few speeches it was time for the choir item, so Russell sidled back to the organ. There he discovered that the Maoris had tidied up so well that they had taken his music with them. The music desk was completely empty with not even a hymn book in sight. Russell left the organ stool and went to grab a book from a chorister so he could at least use a melody line for the anthem, when he noticed a dazed Frank already making his way to the conductor's podium.

Still without music and nowhere near the organ stool, Russell made a frantic 'Cut! Wait!' motion with his hand that Frank interpreted as an 'I am ready to start' signal, so he immediately gave the upbeat. The choir launched in beautifully and after the few seconds it took kangaroo Kent to hop back on the stool, he joined in, playing by memory. At the first modulation, his memory chose to put his fingers in the key of Z-sharp minor while the choir soared away in Qflat major. Miserably, choir and organist cha-cha'd up and down the keys as Frank glared at his organist. Russell decided he should keep going until the end of the piece or he had a coronary, whichever came first.

None of the combatants got to the end. Choir, conductor and organist gave up the struggle and put the listeners as well as themselves out of their misery. They stayed where they were, heads bowed, in defeat. Silence fell until a quick-thinking MC moved to the next event on the programme.

One more simple item remained: *God Save the Queen*. It said so on the service sheet. So why did Frank play *God Defend New Zealand?* And he played it loudly, frantically and determined to make reparation for the rest of the disastrous ceremony. Russell, wishing for the end of the world, at the same time thundered out *God Save the Queen* from memory on the organ and hoped that Frank would see sense and stop. Which, after a few lines of atonal piano-organ screechings mixed with antiphonal bleats from the audience and whimpers from Russell, he did.

Audiences misbehaving

"I thundered: 'SILENCIO'!"

In this short-attention-span, goggle-box-addicted world we inhabit, it is common to see people during concerts behaving as if they were at home in front of television. Audiences forget that not only can others around them hear and see what everyone else is doing, but often, so can the performer. The resident bag lady (a staple member of any audience) will arrive 20 minutes late, work her way to the front row, crackling and rustling. Once seated in the player's eyeline, she will then spend another 20 minutes re-arranging bags and contents; then leave early to avoid the retiring collection.

In a severe case of situational blindness, a workman once appeared at the back of the Town Hall in Auckland during a concert and began blithely hammering. At a church in Milano Marittima, Italy, Martin Setchell's concert programme was accompanied by the joyous sound of money clattering into the offering box at the foot of the statue of Mary.

An overt example of audience insensitivity during a concert by Christopher Herrick at the opening of the Christchurch Town Hall Rieger in 1997 stunned those who saw it. The audience, numbering nearly 2,500, were all pretty much cheek-by-cheque-butt crammed together — we had waited 25 years to hear this concert. In the midst of the throng sat the local village idiot with his copy of the daily newspaper opened wide, turning pages and rustling with relish as he did so. It was surprising that the audience immediately around him did not fix the problem with a swift garrotting. I was planning to take the matter in hand myself at half time when unfortunately the security heavies had him removed and spoiled the fun. (If it is any comfort, this is not a new phenomenon. During the inaugural concert of the Hill organ in Sydney Town Hall in 1890 audience members reported 'prominent citizens' among the rest of the audience talking loudly. After being given a 'hard look' by a lady nearby, one gentleman "had the kindness to stop talking, but commenced whistling."[3])

Back in Christchurch, but at a different concert: the audience of 700 listened, hushed, to Debussy's *Clair de Lune* played by Martin Setchell, and the velvety strings were a mere whisper hanging in the air. No-one stirred. Then a cellphone rang. The owner answered, and chatted to the caller above the music. For several minutes he continued, unaware of dark murmurings around him. I swear I could hear sleeves being rolled up, knives being sharpened. Either the piece or his conversation finished before there was any bloodshed, but he was lucky to escape with his cellphone — not to mention body — intact.

Douglas Lawrence had no qualms at all about what to do with a noisy audience when he was on tour in 2005 with the choir of Ormond College. Organisers of concerts in the old church in Blevio, Como, request that the organ is played, no matter the nature of the concert. So in this mainly choral event Douglas programmed a Frescobaldi toccata, and *Wie schoen leuchtet de Morgenstern* by Buxtehude.

> "About the middle of the Buxtehude the attentive audience was disturbed by an increasingly noisy family at the rear of the church. On the second page of the Buxtehude (remember we were in Italy) I thundered SILENCIO! and indeed silence ensued. After the concert it was 'Bravo Maestro' many times. Ah, Italy."

3 Ampt, *The Sydney Town Hall Organ — William Hill's Magnum Opus*, 24.

Audiences sometimes can not help themselves. Fred Swann was performing with an orchestra in a college auditorium. The organ was positioned on a side wall, just off the stage, literally out in the auditorium, and the instrument had considerable power. The programme began with a Handel concerto, and Fred's registration was appropriately light. The Poulenc concerto followed the Handel.

> "The conductor told me to begin when I was ready, that he would start conducting shortly before the orchestra was to enter. I played the opening chord on full organ, and when I lifted the left hand chord, a woman (obviously very frightened by the unexpected power of the organ) literally screamed '*Oh, My God!*' The audience, conductor, orchestra — all became convulsed with laughter. I stopped, and after decorum was restored I turned to the audience and warned them to brace for a repetition of that opening chord. I can never play that concerto without remembering the incident and listening for a shriek from the audience."

Sean Tucker's self-discipline is admirable. He was playing a lunchtime recital in a large parish church that was concurrently the venue for an art exhibition. Since the building was still open to visitors (and the sidesmen asleep), people were walking around quietly — except for two women, both of whom had failed to notice the large posters by the door advertising an organ recital 'THIS LUNCH-TIME' and the 250 quiet souls seated in the nave.

> "I believe it was during a quiet movement from Widor *Symphony IV* that the silly woman came up to me at the organ console (with her back to the nave) and announced, in a voice like gravel 'Oh Glad! Look — here is the organ-player. Hello! Are you doing a bit of practice, then'?"

In Astorga Cathedral the organ console and the door that leads to it about six metres away can be seen clearly by the audience. It was here that Raúl Prieto Ramírez was in hand-to-hand combat with a piece by Reger when a man in his mid 50s opened the door leading to the console and began to approach. Step by step, as silently as possible, the man edged forward, until he reached the console. Raúl concentrated his energies on Reger and tried to ignore the man, who thrust his concert programme in Raúl's face.

> "With a little voice he asked which piece I was playing at that moment. I could not believe it! Was that a joke? Well, I had to continue playing but I also had to get rid of him, so while I kept playing I hissed: Reger! Of course he might have thought it an insult because I am sure for him it did not matter whether it was Bach, Reger or whatever. But after that short word that sounded like an insult, his face turned happier and he simply went back down to the church benches. It was surreal!"

The main organ in the Cathedral of the Blessed Sacrament in Christchurch is high on the West End gallery. On major occasions the audience has to spill over into the galleries on the same level. Playing the organ part in a performance of Benjamin Britten's *St Nicholas*, Martin Setchell had only one minute and 20 seconds between the end of one organ section and the beginning of the next in which to dash from the small organ downstairs at the front up to the main organ in the back gallery. His route to the gallery organ via a staircase in a colonnade was mapped out and rigorously rehearsed with a stop-watch.

Impressed by these training sessions, the choir had a T-shirt made for him bearing the legend *Champion Organist sprinter — Streaky Setchell proudly sponsored by Dial-an-Organist. From 0 to 50 in 1.20 or your audience back*. Martin proudly wore it during rehearsals. On the night of the performance there were no spare seats in the basilica; the entire ground floor, gallery, and side chapels were as full as fire authorities and common decency would allow. Martin's rehearsed manoeuvre went like a dream as he sprinted from the lower organ, up the colonnade staircase, along the gallery, and weaved through the audience. With time rapidly running out, he arrived to find the organ stool occupied by a couple, enjoying the performance and their prime view. Breathlessly, he asked them to move.

> "Oh no, we have our tickets, we're not shifting now," they said.

> "You have to," said Martin. "I'm the organist and I need to sit here. Now."

They remained firmly on the bench and petulantly demanded to know if Martin had bought a ticket — and presumably the right to that seat. His next entry fast approaching, Martin had no other option but to slide forcefully onto one end of the bench, pushing the surprised pair off the other. He barely had time to draw stops, and find his place before the conductor's downbeat.

Occasionally the audience can be just as entertaining as the performer — if not more so — with spot of pertinent heckling. Barry Jordan heard an organist play the Charles Ives Variations in Ireland. In the preamble the organist mentioned "it is the tune we know as *God save the Queen*."

To which came the very audible response, "No queens in Ireland, dear."

" I donned his shoes and waddled on stage, feeling very much like Bozo the Clown."

Another suitcase, another hall ~ organists on tour

'When you have very bad accident, I want to be fully responsible'

Travelling the world as a concert organist is a unique but hard way to earn a living. It is like performing at home, except the hazards are magnified one hundred-fold and stress-levels raised beyond those recommended by the family doctor. The peripatetic performer's privilege of visiting unexplored territories, and of different sounds, fresh adventures, new friends and lost luggage are off-set by the inevitable difficulties of travel. Even the people designated to look after a touring organist can be as much a liability as a help.

Keith John had had minders before, especially in communist countries which was mostly satisfactory; two registrants provided in Hungary in Cold War days became good friends. But on a later visit to Japan he was surprised to find that the gentleman who had arranged the venture would accompany Keith and his wife the entire time. A meeting at the airport was followed by a good meal and plenty of organ chit-chat, with no hint of the passion to come. Next day on the three-hour Shinkansen journey, it was intense organ chatter again, although Keith wanted only to relax and look out of the window.

"Unfortunately, this became a pattern. Down we would go to breakfast, out would come the laptop and off we would go again. And we had not even got to the concert hall. There were endless explanations of every conceivable facet of the instrument, the building, the atmospheric conditions in the hall, how these could be altered to suit every situation etc. Finally I got to start the long preparations for the full programme I was giving. I had hoped to be left in peace; but no, my minder sat there the whole time, either glued to his laptop or making 'helpful' suggestions. This happened every practice session."

Keith was never left alone. Even at meals the organ chit-chat was relentless, nor was there any chance of a moment or two of glorious silence. One day the minder had business elsewhere and they were free to go exploring. But on his return they had to report on what they had done.

"On the day of the concert, I began to wish I had never heard of the organ but, of course, the adrenalin always flows; it was not bad, but not as good as it could have been. Good public reaction, very complimentary at the CD signing and the reception afterwards, but our friend wasn't quite satisfied because there were a few slips that ruined his recording. The following day on the return train journey he went through the audience reaction papers which he had to admit were better than he had thought! What a relief when he took his leave of us."

Jennifer Bate was assigned a harpsichordist to act as guide and interpreter on one of her tours in Japan.

"He actually spoke very little English, and what he knew had been learned doing a dissertation on mean tone temperament. Over the week, I heard more than I ever wanted to know on the subject. One night, I tried to

> give him the slip, but he spotted me leaving the hotel and insisted on joining me, saying 'When you have very bad accident, I want to be fully responsible'."

Things went a little better for Jennifer when she prepared her debut recital in Vallombrosa Abbey, Italy, and where she was befriended by an English-speaking nun from Rome. When the nun heard that her return journey the following week would mean changing trains in Rome, with an hour's connecting time, she promised that the sisters would bring the convent mini-bus to the station and take Jennifer for a tour of the city.

> "However, my train into Rome ran more than an hour late, so I despaired of catching the next one to Pisa or seeing my friend. I need not have worried. A line of nuns was waiting on the platform. They scooped me and my belongings up and we ran the length of the station to where the Rome to Pisa express was waiting, unable to depart because the guard was being held by four more nuns."

Forgetting to pack items of clothing constitutes a crises if you perform in costume, as Martin Setchell does when he presents his *Bach's Back* concerts. Dressing in formal court clothes of the 18th century means a large suitcase, hose, buckles, constant ironing, washing and frequent inspection of J.S.B.'s wig for hair loss. When we took the programme to Japan I had listed all the components so thoroughly that even the Baroque lice were accounted for.

It was only when the artist's call came for the start of the 'conventional' second half of his concert in the Kitakyushu City Hall in Kokura that I realised Martin's normal winged-collar shirt to go with his tails was hanging, immaculately washed and pressed, in our hotel wardrobe. Martin had no choice but to wear only what he had to hand. Japanese audiences are still shaking their heads over the curious dress sense of the strange Westerner who had performed wearing a cute and frilly 18th century blouse with his 20th century evening tails.

Having shoes specifically designed for playing the organ is vital and without them pedalling can be like skating on flypaper. Street shoes, sneakers and bare feet are not acceptable alternatives, so if you leave your shoes behind, be prepared to fudge that fugue. Felix Hell once forgot his shoes but he was able to borrow a pair from a local lad. The temporary shoes were far more comfortable than his usual ones so he still has them. Presumably the local lad has, in turn, borrowed a pair from second local lad who has borrowed a pair, who has . . .

Proving there is no accounting for taste in the criminal mind, one organist had his organ shoes stolen from the gallery in the Great Hall at the Sydney University just before a concert; luckily he and Robert Ampt take the same size in organ shoes, and a temporary swap ensured his tootsies twinkled through the toccatas.

John Longhurst and Robert (Bob) Cundick had what turned out to be a sole-searching experience when touring Japan as accompanists to the Mormon Tabernacle Choir in Salt Lake City. They were to perform at the NHK Concert Hall in Tokyo, using both the organ and the piano for some of the lighter fare. The pipework and console were located on the side wall, in front of the stage with keydesk and base of the instrument slightly above the stage. Getting from organ to the piano (on stage, of course) was a bit of a hike, involving stairs and getting from stage left to stage right. En route from the hotel to the hall, Bob realised that he had left his organ shoes behind. It was too late to go back; one pair of shoes would have to do for both of them.

> "Fortunately I had the larger feet. My shoes would be a bit roomy for him, but I never could have squeezed my feet into his shoes. As the programme opened, both of us were seated up by the organ console. Bob was to accompany some pieces, I would accompany others. Each time it was the other's turn to mount the bench we would duck down behind the railing during the applause and change shoes. That went quite well, until a point in the programme where I had to move down to the stage dur-

> ing one of Bob's numbers in order to be ready to play the piano for the following selection. That left the organ shoes on Bob's feet, but the shoes I had worn to the hall were far too casual to wear on stage and would have looked ridiculous."

So where was he to find suitable shoes on a moment's notice? They had a choir of 360, so John rapidly sized up the feet of those backstage. The only shoes that could possibly work were those of the associate conductor who had a lovely pair in black patent leather.

> "The only problem was that his feet were at least four sizes larger than mine. It did not matter; there was no other option, so I donned his shoes and waddled on stage, feeling very much like Bozo the Clown. The shoes were so large that they nearly fell off every step I took. They were so long that I could not get my toes onto the piano pedals. So I just pedalled with a large flap of shoe leather extending beyond my toes.
>
> Eventually it came time for the associate conductor to mount the podium. By that time Bob had joined me on the stage for some four-hand piano accompaniments. Realising that we faced a problem I left the stage during the applause, gave the associate back his shoes, put on my organ shoes, and Bob wore his street shoes which, fortunately were at least black and probably weren't too noticeable on stage."

By far the greatest fun can be had when language enters the concert equation. It helps to be good at charades; I have performed impromptu dances such as the little-known Gesticulating Chicken in China (read: 'Where can we get something to eat?') and the more elegant 'The door to the loft is locked' rumba in Warsaw. After observers have recovered from hysterics the message gets through. It would simpler, but less entertaining, if Esperanto was mandatory for itinerant musicians.

David Sanger turned up to play in an historic church in Italy where there had not been an organ recital for many years. Close to the concert starting time a man arrived with a microphone and loudspeaker, and managed to communicate without speaking any English that he was going to announce each piece for the public.

> "He sat in the gallery with me, but too far away for me to be able to attract his attention. He did not seem to understand that some pieces had several movements, and he announced the second piece as I was about to start the second movement of the first piece, and so on. By the time he announced the final item, I was only half way through. That audience must have thought that I played about 20 encores as I gradually worked my way through to the end of the programme."

On another occasion in Norway David was forewarned that the priest who was to thank him did not have a musical ear and understood nothing about music. When David was about to finish a piece mid-way through the programme, his page turner hissed to him to move on quickly as the priest appeared to be getting out of his seat at the front of the church to do the honours. And so on for each piece following. David had to leap from item to item without a pause as the priest was as keen as an Olympic sprinter to be hot off his seat and into the plaudits.

"Sometimes I was forced to start before I had fully prepared the registration, with sometimes disastrous consequences."

If the page turner and organist do not share a language in common, the thrills and spills increase. In a rather scantily-rehearsed 1990 recording with a Canadian Choir on the 19th century organ of the St Joriskirk in Amersfoort, the Netherlands, Christopher Dawes was provided with a page turner and registrant who spoke almost no English, while he spoke almost no Dutch.

> "After realising the gravity of this situation we quickly devised a system to map out the stop knobs for the large baroque organ's three manuals and pedals,

> which were laid out in neat rows and columns (A1, for example, was the knob highest up and furthest to the left, B1 just below it, etc.) Hastily-added (and subsequent to that day, mysterious and useless) markings +G3, -A2, B2+C7, etc. quickly filled my scores, and saved the day."

On a concert trip to Poland in 2003, Gail Archer had even less time in which to prepare for a concert in Holy Family Church, Lublin.

> "It was one of those occasions on which you arrive at the church, they tell you that there is a wedding, some confessions, a Mass, and you have about two hours to prepare your concert on an organ that has only two possible mechanical combinations. If that stress was not enough, the registrant arrived 10 minutes before the concert and could not speak a word of English, Italian or German. I set the whole thing up with two colours of Post-It notes for left or right, and clear numbers for everything, and we just flew by the seat of our pants. It worked, but my heart was beating extra fast, and I bet the tempos were, too."

Being unaware of local customs can cause problems for visiting artists as Roman Krasnovsky from Israel found after his performance in Graz, Austria. The local organist invited Roman to eat with him, his wife, and a large number of their friends at a restaurant.

> "I felt uncomfortable and embarrassed about having the church organist pay for my meal, so even though I was very hungry, I ordered only a cup of coffee. The whole group had a huge meal, a real feast which included all kinds of meats, potatoes, salad, food that smelled great. I was jealous. When we were ready to leave, I gently asked the church organist about my pay

for the concert I gave. He looked at me and said: 'Roman, this meal was your pay'."

Roman continued his gastronomic gaffes when he gave a concert in a small city in Germany.

"After the concert, as usual, we went to a restaurant to celebrate our success. The meal was the best I ever had. I can still remember its taste. During the meal someone came behind me and handed me a guest book and I heard him say: "Mr Krasnovsky, please write something."

So, I wrote: 'A roast beef like this, I never tasted in my entire life.' Then I signed my name and added Shalom in Hebrew. I read out loud what I had written, and right away I felt that something was wrong; people looked at me surprised. I did not understand the problem. The church organist told me: 'Mr Krasnovsky, we gave you the church guest-book and not the restaurant guest-book'."

A noisy noise annoys an organist

"There are not as many people in your audience as I expected. It is very disappointing; we will need to renegotiate your fee."

Part of the attraction of organs comes from the sheer din they can make. And noise equals power. But cautionary word of warning to those wishing to challenge this king of instruments: In a Mine Is Bigger than Yours debate an organist will almost always win.

Such as when the organist was Christopher Herrick in rehearsal for Berlioz's great choral/orchestral Te Deum (an extravagant piece that begins with alternating loud chords from orchestra and organ, supposedly representing the twin powers of the Emperor and the Pope). Christopher, as the Pope at the organ, was pitted against the London Symphony Orchestra. The conductor gave the beat in a relaxed way for the orchestra's opening chord, then, after the pause, in a 'witty' display of disdain for organists in general, he held his nose with one hand and pulled at a pretend toilet flush with the other. Christopher had prepared a genuine full organ sound with everything on that mighty instrument coupled.

> "In those days, before the St Paul's organ had undergone the first of the Mander rebuilds, it was a seriously loud organ sound under the dome, so the conductor's rather scornful action brought forth much more than he

> had reckoned with. Having had his bluff called and been taken by surprise in a big way, he turned to the orchestra and said, 'Right! Beat that!' and he threw himself into a Hoffnung-esque gyration in order to exact every ounce of volume from the poor players. In spite of this display of energy, it is safe to say that the Emperor, however strong and powerful, did not successfully compete with the Pope on that occasion."

Some years ago Douglas Lawrence was rehearsing the Saint-Säens *Organ Symphony* with the Melbourne Symphony Orchestra in the Melbourne Town Hall.

> "Towards the end of the work I thought 'What the hell' and pulled on the 32ft Diaphone, Tuba Mirabilis and other obscenities. As the final chord died away the conductor, Leonard Dommett, called up to the organ 'Mr Lawrence, this evening I shall simply wave a white flag'."

Insensitive visitors to the loft are sure to inflame an organist's annoyance glands. In the late 1990s David Rumsey was preparing a recital on an Australian cathedral organ that had a disastrous pedal department. It was almost entirely borrowed from the Great and was thwarting him.

> "This was agony, since little but duplicated notes were my unhappy lot and I desperately needed them to sound. Up strode a character to the console (roped off, I might add) and announced he was an English organ builder with the greeting 'Hello, just visiting, how are you?' and everything else that you do not want to hear when time is short and problems are manifest.
>
> It was the most inappropriate moment imaginable to be interrupted and I continued working hoping he would take the hint. But he was utterly insensitive to this and kept chatting. There was nothing to do but be patient, continuing to set up as best I could. He proudly told me

> that it was he who, in England years ago, had first had the bright idea of endowing otherwise completely mechanical organs with an electric action pedal division borrowed from the Great."

Church authorities making capital on the sly are not appreciated. British pianist and organist, William (Bill) Davies had been employed by a church to open one of Hill, Norman and Beard's new organs and Frank Fowler was sent by the company to stand by in case of emergency.

> "The church authorities had asked the company to reimburse them for Bill's recital fee as a donation, which we were daft enough to do. When I walked into the church Bill was rehearsing *Tico Tico* to show the versatility of the organ to the authorities.
>
> Just before the recital Bill went out for a smoke in the car park and I went with him. I told him jokingly that as the company were paying his fee they had sent me down to see we got our money's worth. Bill was horrified, not at what I had said, but because he was giving his services to the Church and making no charge — and people sometimes wonder that after having spent some 48 years working in churches I am, on occasions, a bit cynical."

It would have been entirely understandable if David Aprahamian Liddle had decided he would rather be sticking needles under his fingernails than continue with one particular organ concert, but his professionalism got him through. David was in Maine to give a concert, and was at the mercy of a tactless host who was oblivious to life's little courtesies such as letting doors shut in David's face.

Nevertheless, David survived to the concert, and after the interval, as he was settling back at the console to play the second half, his host approached him.

> "David, there are not as many people in your audience as I expected. It is very disappointing; we will need to renegotiate your fee."

Church organists will be familiar with this little scenario: they have ignited the souls of worshippers with aptly chosen and beautifully played pre-service voluntaries, only to have the verger douse them with his clarion announcement of a trivial detail. David Sadler recounts an inflammatory variation on this at King Edward's School, Birmingham, when the organist was playing as parents and prize-winners assembled in readiness for Speech Day, a grand occasion held in Big School.

> "On to the platform marched a rather feared and fiery-tempered modern languages master, a former monk but nonetheless peppery of speech when easily irked by boys, colleagues or even the Chief Master. Vain attempts to silence the offending organ music by waving his arms increased his frustration and fury. Suddenly his temper was cast from its insecure moorings: 'OH DO STOP THAT NOISE.' When stunned silence fell he announced calmly, but still red-faced from his exertions, 'Would the owner of car number so and so please be aware that you've left your lights on.' Silent, seething anger was evident from the console aloft."

Thanks to a thoughtful electrician, Barry Jordan has kept his body and soul together by making tea and fish-cakes in the loft during the Good Friday vigil.

In Church

How to survive a sermon without waking others

"I could get out at the start of the sermon, get a cup of tea and a bacon sandwich, then be back in time for the end of the intercessions"

More organists are to be found scuttling around churches than concert halls, principally because of the history of the instrument. For many people the very word organist conjures up visions of a moustachioed Aunty Fred pedalling an asthmatic harmonium. Most of us who play the organ have had to offer our services in church for no other reason that our mothers at least knew where to find us.

We continue to play because it offers the impecunious muso a trade-off for an instrument on which to practise, or in some instances, a genuine desire to serve. Money does not usually motivate organists to take up church positions, and neither do the working conditions of freezing temperatures, hard organ benches and interminable ramblings from frequently inarticulate worthies. Directly connected to the latter, there are rumoured to be at least

50,000 organs worldwide sporting a well-used Open Pulpit Trapdoor stop. Although the organists' unofficial motto is 'Practise while he preaches' by all accounts practice is way down the list of favoured sermon activities.

The first line of defence is to avoid the sermon altogether. At Sean Tucker's church it is the custom for the choir to leave before the sermon. Taking it in turns, one of the organists then returns to finish the rest of the service. That is the theory — but like all good theories it can collapse with embarrassing results.

> "Once, years ago, my previous Director of Music and his assistant were both deep in conversation after letting the choir out. They continued in conversation to the car-park and carried on for some minutes, when one of them said, 'Shouldn't one of us be in church on the organ bench?' I can't remember if he made it back in time."

Sean was once caught out at Evensong when both organists had gone out with the choir as usual. But this time the Rector decided to preach for about four minutes only. As Sean returned, the church was silent and one of the choir was frantically gesticulating and mouthing: "He has finished — the hymn — QUICK!"

> "The only option was to walk carefully to the centre of the stalls, bow reverently to the high altar and then proceed to the organ console where, for some unknown reason, I bowed again; then I got on and played the hymn over. With no stops drawn. . ."

After a brief panic Sean realised his mistake.

> "I quickly pressed a general piston (forgetting that I had previously re-set it for some other item) and played the quiet evening hymn over on tutti reeds and cornets. At that point anyone else in church, who had been asleep, also woke up."

If you cannot avoid the sermon, come prepared. Hunger, particularly for small boys, plays a large part in deciding how to pass the time. Adrian Taylor had a church post with the organ console in full view, smack in the middle of the choir stalls.

> "I had a well-trained chorister whom I could despatch to the local tea rooms to order me a bacon sandwich (before the service), so I could get out at the start of the sermon, get my cup of tea and sandwich, then be back in time for the end of the intercessions. It was particularly handy the morning after a few pints."

Organ lofts with the spaciousness of a wet-suit present difficulties for anything wildly athletic, but providing an innovative soul has organised a sensibly positioned power point, there is no limit to the entertainments available. Thanks to a thoughtful electrician, Barry Jordan has kept his body and soul together by making tea and fish-cakes in the loft during the Good Friday vigil.

Doughnuts were a favourite sermon-enhancer for one cathedral organist who reminisced about his younger, less responsible days:

> "At Winchester one of us used to pop out of the loft and go over to the mini-supermarket on Sunday morning for a bag of doughnuts to eat during the sermon. Very nice they were too, but the keys got a bit sticky."

In case it seems this inattention to The Word is a sign of the modern atheist society we live in, I should point out that trotting off for a refreshment mid-sermon was cultivated centuries ago in many a cathedral or church where the position of the console enabled the organist to make a discreet getaway. At Holy Trinity, Hull, more than 50 years ago, the organist would sometimes quietly go down from the console and slip out of the north door into the Bonny Boat for a swift half pint. Tom Cawthra, the organist of St Bartholomew's, Armley, Leeds between 1878 and 1921, regularly timed his communion with the spirit world to perfection. Tom spent the half-hour sermons during Evensong at the Maltshovel pub, courtesy of the back door of the organ.

Others have taken the chance to make a quick escape. George Guest used to go up to the organ loft after the anthem and say to the organ scholar "You play them out — I have to get ready for Hall." He would then disrobe and slip across to the Baron of Beef for a couple of pints.

For some organists, alcohol hindered rather than helped their performance. Lincoln Cathedral records noted that Thomas Kingston, organist from 1599 to 1616, reported another organist was "verye often drunke and by means there of he hathe by unorderlye playing on the organs putt the quire out of time and disordered them."[4] He would not be the only one.

Having satisfied the inner soul, with the pulpit incumbent mid-stream and with time to grind on, the musicians then have to amuse themselves. After reading the Sunday *Independent*, one bored organist admits that he finds it a mildly diverting pastime to play the very top notes on the Swell Piccolo 2ft quietly to simulate hearing aid noises.

In an idle moment between sermonic ums and ers, Sean Tucker discovered that both Salisbury Cathedral and Sherborne Abbey had cameras that are controllable from the organ console.

> "When playing at either building, I found it entertaining to move the cameras around the congregation during the sermon, in order to see if there was any 'hot totty' as it were, in the throng. Just occasionally, one would be rewarded with the sight of some flaxen-haired beauty, looking as if she had come from a TV advertisement set, promoting hair or skin products. More usually, though, there was only a collection of old people looking as if they had just come from a badger-baiting session."

Sean was once assistant to an organist who used to smoke in the north choir aisle, near the console, during the sermon.

---

4 Lindsay, *An Encyclopedia of Quotations about Music*, 128.

> "If he was not smoking there, he and I used to sit in the Lady Chapel, with the monitor speaker just high enough to hear when the mumbling ceased, and discuss whatever topic came to mind. Now I often use the time to do some marking or other school preparation. I also occasionally do some work for my Russian lessons. Often, though, I just sit and read a book."

In modern times a discreetly hidden earplug can harbour the latest iPod pop single, or a Test match special during the cricket season. But all scientific advancement is not necessarily progress in the minds of reluctant sermon-sitters. Robert Bowles laments the introduction of reliable sound reinforcement systems that have done away with the more physical declamatory style of preaching — which in turn means that playing cricket during the sermon is no longer possible. He explains:

> "As a chorister (some 45 years ago) I must also have heard many excellent sermons, but the content was a bit over our heads. The answer, for those who could see the preacher, was to play cricket. Before the service one agreed with one's neighbour who would be which team, and who would bat first. From the start of the sermon, both players would observe the gestures of the preacher very closely, and interpret each one as one of the standard signals given by cricket umpires to the scorer.
>
> For example, arms outstretched horizontally meant a wide (one run); both arms raised towards heaven (six runs); hand moving to and fro horizontally (four runs); a hand with a finger pointing forward and waved up and down admonishing the transgressors, (batsman out). After the service you compared notes to see if you finished up with the same score. One particular preacher, when talking about nuclear disarmament, would regularly generate a score of both teams all out for no runs; but his sermons were understandable to 11 year-olds, so one could listen instead."

Impromptu glissandi from the organ during sermons are often the result of organists reaching for a hymn book or heavy bound music volume which they have accidentally dropped on the top manual. The Law of Physics decrees that all objects landing on an organ keyboard will slide with great effect to the bottom manual, and that all stops will be drawn at the time. If small enough, the objects will continue to fall, landing between the keys of the pedal board. Colin Mitchell rates his most embarrassing blunder as the time he dropped a hymn-book that bounced down four manuals prepared for the final hymn.

> "That was bad enough, but trying to retrieve it from the pedals, I slipped, banged my head and went cassock over surplice, landing on all fours on something approaching full pedal."

Keith John painfully recalls that he was rewarded with a beating when he made a similar mistake:

> "While at the King's School, Gloucester, I used to play the organ in the Cathedral for the short daily morning service. One day during the prayers before my final blaze of glory at the end on full organ, I was taking the chunky hymn book off the music desk when it slipped and slithered all the way down the four manuals; it made a tremendous noise (Ligeti would have been proud) and there was rather a long silence before prayers resumed. Afterwards, I was summoned to see the senior master to explain myself; all my efforts to convince this stupid man, who had no artistic sense whatsoever, that the almighty noise was the result of a genuine accident failed. Result: I received a painful six of the best."

For some, the sermon is an ideal time to do some swift warm-ups for the impending anthem. One organist was settling down for the Word at a well-attended Easter service and decided on some incidental finger exercises.

> "I started out practising silently, decided I had done enough, set a fairly vigorous registration to announce the next hymn, read for a few minutes, got bored, forgot what I had done already (the fatal mistake of setting the next registration), decided 'I'll get in a little more practice', launched into the opening bar of the Tournemire-Duruflé *Victimae Paschali Laudes*. It startled the heck out of everyone, not least he of the reversed collar. I am not one for setting registrations too early these days."

Former Director of the Royal School of Church Music Lionel Dakers would regale students at the RSCM Addington Palace summer course with the story of a former organist of Westminster Abbey who played in carpet slippers that he kept secured to his feet by elastic. One fell off during a sermon so he bent down to pick it up, misjudged the angle, and spreadeagled across the pedals. Naturally, stops were drawn for the next hymn, and not being particularly athletic, the organist struggled to clamber back up again, all the while parping and honking his way up and down the 32ft Double Ophecleide and Bombardes.

Catching up on sleep is not only a viable option but one that is often unavoidable for hard-working musicians. During his college years, after an especially late night of partying, Todd Wilson was unable to keep his eyes open.

> "So I lay down on the floor behind the organ bench for a short rest during the sermon. After the sermon, despite repeated (and ever louder) announcements of the closing hymn, I remained fast asleep and the congregation finally left in silence. Though this was many years ago, I can still recall the unnerving sensation of being gently nudged awake by choir members staring down at me asking 'Todd, are you alright'?"

Colin Mitchell recounts what he hopes is a true tale of an incident at St Paul's Cathedral, when John Stainer was organist there. The story goes that he fell soundly asleep during the sermon, and on waking up, discovered to his horror that the choir were singing the last verse of the last hymn without him.

> "With great presence of mind, he very softly joined in with quiet foundations, drew more and more stops, and brought the hymn to a thunderous conclusion, as all eyes focused on the organ console. After playing the final voluntary, Stainer left the console, wandered down to the choir vestry, removed his robes and put on his overcoat as the choir remained robed and silent. With great style, Stainer put on his gloves, picked up his music-case, made towards the door, opened it, and then turned back, saying 'Thank you so much gentlemen. A splendid final hymn, and just the way I wanted it. Good morning.' With that he departed without another word."

To be fair, sermons are not the only danger points for somnolent souls; follow a heavy night with the siesta time of an Evensong the next day, and you have a perfect recipe for trouble. Jeremy Filsell did not wait until the sermon to succumb when he was accompanying a choir in Chichester Cathedral singing Howells' Collegium Regale canticles at Evensong.

> "The organ loft at Chichester was then on the central screen and I remember lying down on the floor during the first lesson to gaze up at the bosses on the central tower. They were the last things I recall seeing as I went out. The next thing I knew was the end of the Creed being said downstairs as I awoke; having slept throughout the Nunc Dimittis, my mea culpas afterwards were copious. I later learnt that the pregnant pause after the lesson had finally been interrupted by the tenor soloist beginning the Nunc sans orgue: Howells' Nunc was thus sung, perhaps for the first time ever, entirely a capella."

Kimberly Marshall tells the story of the late Herbert Nanney, who was the university organist at Stanford for most of his career, playing thousands of weddings during his time there (sometimes at

9 am, 11 am, 1 pm, 3 pm, 5 pm and 7 pm on a single Saturday). Eventually fatigue caught up with him and he fell asleep not during a sermon or a lesson, but nothing less than a full-blooded processional — which he was playing at the time. He woke up, hands still on a chord and calmly continued playing. No one said anything to him about it, so he never knew how long they heard that D major chord on full organ.

Diversifying mid-sermon entertainments is possibly the best way to go. Colin Mitchell has the most varied of loft sermon-time activities that any organist has admitted to. He has:

- Fed a hamster in a box
- Slept
- Put new points in the car distributor
- Read a book
- Drawn cartoons
- Spilled aniseed balls on the pedals
- Polished the console woodwork
- Cleaned the keys and stop-heads
- Replaced pedal light bulbs
- Practised silent voluntaries
- Polished his shoes
- Gone to the pub for a pint

Not all organists can escape from their ecclesiastical cages during the service. Elderly players suffer in particular. At an inner city church where he played, Neil Shilton says the organist was trapped in an enclosure and could not get out while the minister was preaching — which he did for a considerable time.

> "I played for only about six services at this church but I quickly noticed an odour about the organ console. After some discreet enquiries from an old organist I found that it was not uncommon, during a long sermon, for the organist to relieve himself between the pedals."

At the opposite extreme, the heights of sophistication to which sermon-activities can rise are astonishing. David Rumsey has experienced some of the best from old hands: church musicians in Denmark, where almost all organists and many choristers are professional. They sing from the western galleries, where the organs are placed, but like their Parisian counterparts, do tend to come and go a little during the services, especially the choristers, who occasionally juggle two nearby performances.

> "Sermons are often quite long affairs in Denmark, so this coming and going could sometimes even extend to visits to a nearby inn. Before the 1960s it was always a risky affair to judge when to return for the hymn after the sermon, but later in one church where I was peripherally involved, a new wireless sound installation was acquired (ostensibly for the hearing impaired).
>
> But these are musicians — creative people — of which we speak. Its coverage was soon found to broadcast effectively as far as the local inn. The preacher always ended his sermon with a long prayer. This was the cue to settle accounts and get back to the gallery. On a certain Sunday, however, he launched straight into announcing the next hymn. You can imagine the scramble and the innkeeper's panic as almost all of his clients tore out, clutching 'hearing aids', without paying.
>
> Whether revenge or precaution I do not know, but about this time I was invited to a Christmas party in the back of the organ during the sermon. Then almost everybody smoked — even Danish women sometimes enjoyed pipes or cigars. The priest somehow realised what was happening. He later commented to the effect that he was surprised his preaching had created so much smoke from the gallery. Everybody agreed that it was a whole new concept in fire and brimstone sermons."

In the 1970s and in pre-video days, it was frustrating to listen to the preacher grind through a long address at Evensong that was supposed to go from 7 pm to 8 pm, knowing the best slot of the TV week on television (in this case, *War and Peace*) started at 8 pm. My own solution was to launch the thunderous organ blowers for the final hymn at 7.55 pm, whether the preacher had finished or not, using the rocket launching noises to signal an impending hymn play-over, and with any luck, silence the preacher.

Christopher Herrick was more direct; he admits that he enjoyed the 'power' he had in the organ loft — and he was not afraid to wield it. When he was Dykes Bower's assistant at St Paul's Cathedral in London he put this asset to admirable use:

> "Organists are exposed to an unfair share of sermons, and in my experience many of them were rather silly. In contrast, some were sublime and memorable, not least Martin Luther King when he preached from the St Paul's pulpit. On another occasion a visiting preacher was making the most of his 'moment of fame', drearying on and on and on. This gentleman also had the habit of leaving long, rather random pauses between phrases.
>
> Finally I had had enough, so in one of these pauses I plunged in with the play-over of the next hymn. The choir and clergy sprang to their feet with relief, sang the hymn extra lustily, and I became the hero of the hour."

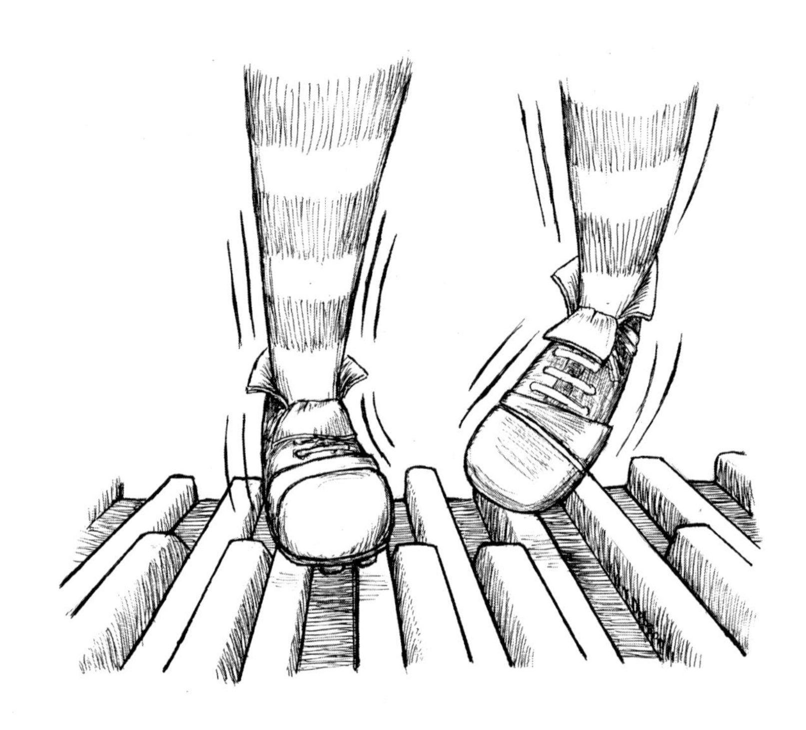

. . . the family was determined to acknowledge the lad's passion for football by asking for the anthem sung at all football games

They wanted what?

"Does anyone know where I can find the music to Delibes Flower Duet? I have to play it in three minutes!"

Funerals and weddings are the meat and drink for musicians so it is not surprising that most church organists of any status claim to have seen it all, one way or another — interminable services, missing or errant key players in the drama, weird music choices, hysterical families and once, a stolen hearse. Some funerals come close to making alcoholics out of even the most sanguine church musician and the necessarily short advance warning for most funerals adds to the explosive potential. Light the blue touch paper and stand well back.

Kerry Beaumont at Coventry Cathedral was asked to play for a funeral at which the family wanted Tchaikovsky's *Waltz of the Flowers* from the *Nutcracker Suite* during the service. Or so he thought.

> "But when I looked in the programme after the service had started I saw, to my horror, that it was the *Flower Duet* from the Delibes opera Lakmé. Frantically I tried to recall the piece to mind during the reading, but I could not find enough to make even a start.

> As soon as the sermon started I rushed down to the cathedral basement to check the internet to see if I could download the score in some form. Every site I accessed either wanted my life story to subscribe or some substantial funds, or both. I gave up and ran over to my flat next to the cathedral to see if I could find it in my miscellaneous sheet music collection but, because I had recently moved in, the music was scattered among many boxes so I gave up."

In desperation Kerry shouted, to no-one in particular, "Does anyone know where I can find the music to Delibes Flower Duet? I have to play it in three minutes!" Kerry's daughter emerged from her room with it on a CD which Kerry thrust gratefully into a player. Poking the widgets into his ears, he forwarded it to the right track as he ran back to the cathedral and the organ console.

> "As I negotiated the three staircases and crossed the ante-chapel area towards the console, the long recitative that precedes the well-known duet was in full swing in my ears. I didn't have time to fast forward it, knowing that it was likely to jump to the next track if I did. Then, to my dismay, I sensed the numbing silence of a post-sermonic gap. The congregation and priest were waiting for me to begin, so I jumped on the organ bench as the recitative ended, and pulled out some hopeful registration just as the recorded singers began the duet."

As he listened to the two sopranos sing through the earpieces, Kerry relayed the duet onto the keyboard as it unfolded. As an added complication, the CD rendition he was listening to was in sharp-studded B major, so his version contained some innovative interpretive notes, but he kept going until the duet, and the agony, ended.

> "My version of the duet coincided with theirs on a few points but, thank God, it came off. Afterwards, people said it was a lovely solo. If they knew how close I

> was to playing absolute gobbledegook they might have been less complimentary."

At the other end of the socially convoluted scale, there were few niceties for a funeral in a church bordering a council tower block somewhere in England. Kick-off was due at 11 am. By 11.05 there was no sign of the family, so a funeral bearer was sent to the tower block address to find them. Next, observers at the church watched as a large fire engine sped past them and turned off in the direction of the tower block. Those already at the church stood and looked at each other. Eventually the funeral bearer returned with the news that "the family had got stuck in the bastard lift, mate".

It transpired that the lift was suitable for a maximum of six people; indeed there were six, but since one of the six weighed 34 stone the mechanism had decided that enough was enough and ground to a halt for the day, getting stuck on the 14th floor. The fire brigade winkled them out, and the funeral service got cracking, an hour and a half late.

Despite even the most determined efforts, it is still possible to trip up. D'Arcy Trinkwon found the Scottish accent so difficult to understand that it got him into a spot of linguistic trouble. He had been asked to play the organ at the funeral of a young Scot. Barely 30, the dead man had been an avid football supporter and regularly attended all major football events. D'Arcy, then only in his mid 20s, knew, and still knows, nothing whatever about football. The grieving family had been invited to the church to discuss music for the service. The vicar felt it would be helpful if D'Arcy met them to discuss their choice of music.

> "It is not the easiest of things to sit in front of a number of family members who are crying and distraught at their loss, especially when you are young and not so experienced with death. I tried my best to remain calm or not to show my embarrassment. Their thick Glasgow accent was made even more unintelligible to my ears as it was heavily weighed down by sorrow."

D'Arcy made a supreme effort to be both professional and comforting while trying to understand what they were saying. He dutifully wrote down the hymns and before-service music they wanted. For the musical interlude the family was determined to acknowledge the lad's passion for football by asking for the anthem sung at all football games.

> "To anyone more worldly-wise than me, the name of this piece may well have been obvious, but I did not know it, so I wrote down exactly what I thought they had said and continued. At the end of the discussion I read out the chosen pieces: Hymn X, Hymn Y, and then the musical interlude *You'll Never Walk Again*.

A hush fell. The family glared angrily at D'Arcy, their eyes filling with tears. He was confused — what had he said wrong?

> "Stunned by this sudden turn of aggression towards me, I was saved by the vicar, who, to defuse the obviously difficult situation, told the family to excuse me as I didn't know anything about football."

After the family had left, the vicar gently educated the bemused D'Arcy. "I think you will find that the name of that song they want you to play is called *You'll Never Walk Alone*."

A favourite past-time for organists is to exchange notes on the worst or most insane pieces ever asked for at a funeral. Requests can border on the bizarre; it is often rumoured that *Smoke Gets in Your Eyes* has been used at crematorium services, but I have yet to hear it first-hand. On demand, I once rollicked my way through *Hello Dolly* for a woman (called Dolly, admittedly) but the family had probably not thought much further than the first line; was it imagination or was there a slight gulp en masse when the line 'You're lookin' swell, Dolly' rang out? One organist was asked for, and played, *Wish me luck as you wave me goodbye*. Gerard Brooks feels he must surely head the field with *I feel good, I knew I would* by the late, great James Brown. On his advice, a CD recording was played instead.

James Welch was invited to play for a memorial at a mortuary in Palo Alto. When he asked if the family wished for any special music, the funeral director said that they wanted *Grand Canyon Suite*.

> "I thought it was an odd request, but I took along my copy of *On the Trail*, the only music from that suite that I owned. When I arrived, I asked someone in the family about any requests. Again they said *Grand Canyon Suite*." I said, 'Yes, that and probably other music as well?' They said 'No, just *Grand Canyon Suite*.' So I played *On the Trail* for about 20 minutes of prelude. Everyone seemed to be happy, but it was a lot of donkey braying at that funeral."

Adrian Taylor can probably boast the most ludicrous music choice. Arriving to play for a funeral, he was greeted by a mildly anxious vicar.

> "There is good news, and bad news: the deceased has apparently left explicit musical requests. He wants *Always look on the bright side of life* (from the Monty Python film *The Life of Brian*) as the coffin goes out."
>
> "Right . . ."
>
> "And I couldn't find a CD."
>
> "Right..."
>
> "I have found the words and the guitar tab — can you play it and sing it at the end?"
>
> "Errr..."

So that is how it came to be that Adrian found himself, in front of the church, dutifully singing 'Life's a piece of shit, when you look at it. . .' as the pallbearers shouldered their burden.

Wirelessly connecting the thought processes of clergy and their organists would save many a hiccough. At the end of the first verse and chorus of *How Great Thou Art* during a funeral service in Auckland, the minister was sure he heard his name being called. He searched the faces of the congregation but could not see anyone looking at him expectantly. After the second verse and chorus, the same thing happened. Although convinced he was experiencing some kind of divine calling, the minister decided instead of replying 'Speak, Lord, your servant is listening', he went, during the third verse, to ask the son of the deceased if he had been trying to get his attention. No, but he had heard something too. When the third verse and chorus came to an end, they heard no name, but as everyone drew a breath for the final verse nothing happened — the organist had stopped. Light dawned. The organist had been trying to attract the minister's attention, wanting to know how many verses were being sung because the words the congregation were singing differed from those in the hymn book. The minister hurriedly announced the last verse, and waited another day for divine intervention.

Usually the hiccoughs come one at a time. But not for Mark Quarmby in Sydney, Australia, for whom God must have decreed that everything, simply everything, would go wrong on one day. And that was despite the best intentions and years of experience. Mark even remembers the year (1999) and month (June). It was the worst funeral he ever played. Probably the worst funeral anyone has played.

> "It all started the evening before, as I was about to play for Evensong at Sydney Cathedral. A colleague of mine rang me to see if I could play for a funeral the following morning, which he was unable to do. I was free so I agreed. The funeral was at 10 am in a Catholic

church a few suburbs away. My friend stressed that I should be there no later than 9.45 am, as there would be a visiting priest taking the funeral. There would be one hymn, *All things bright and beautiful.* Knowing from experience that Catholic churches have no idea what a hymn book is, I packed mine with the required hymn book-marked.

The following morning I walked into the open church on time, but I was surprised to find that there was no coffin, no congregation and no priest. By 9.50 I was beginning to worry, so I rang my colleague, only to get his answering machine. I walked around the altar, hoping I might set off an alarm to get someone's attention. I decided to go outside to see if I could find somebody. Perhaps the funeral was at 10.30 or 11 am?"

Right on 10 am a young girl came running over from the school attached to the church. Waving her arms about as if playing a keyboard in mid-air, she called out that there had been a mix-up and Mark had been told the wrong church; the funeral was at a church in a neighbouring suburb. "They are waiting for you," she yelled.

"Having played for a couple of weddings in this other church some time ago, I had a rough idea where it was; not on the main road, but down a narrow side street, on a hill overlooking the harbour. I ran back inside the church, grabbed my music bag and ran to my car. It was not until I was approaching the next suburb that I realised that I had left the previous organ unlocked and switched on. When I later told this story to a Catholic organist, he laughed and said not to worry; they would not notice for at least six months."

Ten minutes later Mark was looking for somewhere to park his car in the crowded main street of the neighbouring harbour-side suburb. Finally he had to park illegally, Parisian-style, on a street corner. The sign "To Catholic Church" pointed to the side street so he ran down the street, almost into Sydney harbour. But no sign of the church until he looked up to his right and saw the historic stone church above him on the top of the hill. (He later discovered that someone had helpfully bent the sign to point down the wrong street.)

> "What was I to do? I did not have time to run back up the hill and find the correct street. There was no alternative but to scale the cliff through the bush, music bag and all. No sooner had I stepped into the bush than something rustled around my feet. I didn't want to know if I had stepped on a snake. I took off and by the time I got to the top, I was dripping with perspiration, even though it was mid-winter.
>
> "As I ran across the lawn the undertakers were smiling. I must have looked a strange sight appearing from the bushes over the cliff's edge. The funeral director handed me an order of service, saying that they had started without me. It was 10.15 am. I noticed the hymn was first. Had they sung it unaccompanied or left it out? I entered the church and discovered that it was packed. Every aisle, except the central one, was full with standing mourners.
>
> Going down the side aisle, I had to squeeze past countless people. Everyone was looking at me as I repeated 'Excuse me' over and over. I remembered the electronic organ console was in the left transept and I was stunned to find the area, including around the console, packed with people standing. I fought my way to the console, sweat still dripping from my forehead, and collapsed onto the organ bench.
>
> It was locked. I couldn't believe it. I tried to remember where the key was hidden the last time I played here.

Then it came to me. It was hung on a nail behind the hymn number board beside the altar."

Once again Mark had to "s'cuse me, s'cuse me" through the crowd up to the altar. Sure enough, the key was there so he squeezed his way back to the console, unlocked the cover and pushed the ON button. No power. He got off the bench and looked for the power cord and a power point to plug it in to as the nonplussed congregation watched in silence.

> "As soon as I turned it on the priest announced the second hymn that no-one had told me about. I grabbed the order of service to find it was the 23rd Psalm to *Crimond*. I jumped back on the bench and with no time to select any stops, pushed number four of the five general pistons, believing it would be one notch softer than full organ, and would be loud enough to accompany the packed church. What I had not realised was that these general pistons were blind; that is, there was no way of knowing which stops were on and which were off. Moreover, changing any stops by hand made no difference whatsoever to the stop combinations that had been set up internally."

Mark launched into the hymn, playing from memory, and nearly fell off the bench at the noise that blasted from the speakers. It sounded as though some Star Wars character was about to appear on the overhead projector screen, and the console ready to lift off and rise above the congregation.

> "It was impossible to sing along with such a merry-go-round sound, and it took me two verses to set the stops manually while I was playing, and then switch off the general piston I had pushed. No doubt the tremulants got rid of some cobwebs."

The priest began his eulogy with an apology for telling the organist the wrong church, and as the eulogy continued, a large dog bounded down the central aisle and ran round the coffin barking. After the priest finished he announced what should have been the first hymn. Mark flung open the hymn book, only to find it would not stay open. With commendable presence of mind, he grabbed a pile of MIDI discs that were lying on the console and used them as a page holder. As Mark prepared to play Handel's *Largo* for the recessional he felt a tap on his shoulder. They were going to use a recorded track so would he please not play? The coffin was carried out to Frank Sinatra singing *I Did It My Way*.

After all his efforts, Mark discovered that no-one had thought about paying the organist, and he got no fee at the church. A week later he received a cheque for 50% more than he was expecting. Later still, he found the order of service in his music bag, noticing for the first time the dead man's surname: Tale. And so it was . . .

Beware the Brides (and their mothers) of March

"With right-hand and pedals, and a baby balanced precariously on my left arm, I played through the Lohengrin March and then the first hymn"

Weddings can be a sustained torture if there is debate about the music between the couple and (usually) the bride's mother. A sure sign of trouble is when the mother-of-the-bride, rather than either of the couple, phones the organist to arrange their music. One garrulous mama who contacted me for a wedding clearly regarded organists as mere servants at a dynastic match ceremony. She was keen to establish her knowledge of the church and the right to direct operations.

> "Oh yarrss, St Baarnaabaas, I kneoow it weelll," she wah-wahed down the phone on her first call. "Whaay, I drive past it praacticaally every daay."

Interviews with prospective brides are full of surprises. James Welch had a consultation with a bride and her mother. In demonstrating prelude music, he played *Jesu, Joy of Man's Desiring*. The bride and her mother looked at each other, wincing, and told him, "Oh, no, not that! That sounds like church!" He excused himself from that job.

As prime targets for trouble, given that they entail a great deal of planning and a disproportionate amount of money (very little of which ends up with the organist) weddings brim with potential for disaster. Late brides, missing bouquets (and occasionally missing brides and grooms), bizarre music choices, family tensions, weather, and alcohol all play their part.

Occasionally musicians have to work hard to ensure they are not made to look silly. David Pitches was asked to play for a wedding at a church where the organ had not been used for some time and was not in the healthiest condition. While he was playing over the wedding music to the couple a few days before the Big Day to demonstrate how it would sound, the Great reservoir sprang a leak that resulted in a banshee-like wail from a vibrating flap of errant leather.

> "On the morning of the wedding things were so bad that I had to send a member of the choir off to the local hardware shop with a list of emergency repair items, including duct tape and superglue, and as the congregation was gathering I had the unenviable task of crawling around the innards of the organ in my best suit trying to plug air leaks.
>
> About five minutes before the bride arrived, the ivory fell off the Great middle C key. Faced with the extreme discomfort of playing a keyboard with this crucial ivory missing, I decided to fix it by smearing it liberally with superglue. Bad mistake — I ended up with half the Great keys and my 10 fingers covered in superglue. With the bridal party arriving, there was no time to clean up. Amazingly after that, the organ got through the service without a hitch, though I vowed never to play that particular instrument again."

The choice of music is an entertaining battleground. Paul Derrett amicably managed to convince one bride and her mother that *I whistle a happy tune* from *The King and I* was not entirely appropriate given that the song is about being afraid. "That, and the fact that the word 'erect' appears very near the beginning. Appropriate for the day, maybe — appropriate for the service, no."

William (Bill) Sharrow got caught in the crossfire before a wedding, with a surprising outcome. While selecting music with the future bride and groom, Bill played three possible processions for coming in. The bride said she loved the first one and had always dreamed of having that procession at her marriage. The groom mumbled a little that he disliked it, but if that was what she wanted, no problem.

> "Then I played three possible Processions Out. The bride picked number three and once again said that was the one she always dreamed about. 'I hate that piece of music,' replied the groom. 'Look, I okayed that other piece you wanted, and now it is my turn.' I quietly turned off the organ, closed the console, and sent them both back to the priest for more counselling. The wedding never happened. Another divorce saved by the organist."

With luck, the battle ground is more of a playground. In a church in Auckland, an attractive female gym instructor was to marry an extremely handsome male gym instructor. The organist, one of the male instructor's clients, told her sternly that her chosen theme tune from *Superman* was inappropriate and would not work on the organ. Then, with the groom's connivance, he practised it up for the day. Only the minister David Clark could see the bride's ecstatic face when the organist began the theme.

It is little wonder that organists amuse themselves by playing the odd surreptitious ditty. An understandably anonymous player has admitted to serenading wedding guests with *I'm forever blowing bubbles* at the wedding of an older couple, and Andy Lumsden has improvised in a French style on *Rhubarb and Custard* before the bride arrived.

In 1950s rural England, the limited ability of the 10-year-old conscripted organist resulted in a bridal couple marching in, and out, to the theme tune of the popular BBC radio programme, *The Archers*. Another pair obliviously signed the register to the thinly disguised lilt of the 1950 film theme to *Robin Hood* because the organist had lost the key to the music cupboard, and was so unnerved by the experience that she could not play anything else from memory.

In command of an electronic organ for a civil partnership ceremony, Colin Mitchell was startled to see that most of the guests came cross-dressed as nuns. The verve with which they sang filled Colin with admiration.

> "To a man or woman, they stayed with me, and sang every show-tune vigorously, complete with dramatic gestures; the *Sound of Music* medley a cross between *Sister Act* and *Nuns on the Run* with a hint of *The Pope Must Die* due to the fact that most of the real women, dressed in suits, looked and behaved like members of the mafia. Perhaps the highlight was receiving a kiss on the cheek from the 'Mother Superior' as I played the wedding march, 'her' lyrical tenor voice heartfelt as she said, 'Thanks chuck, that wer' smashin'."

It could have been worse. In Wolverhampton, for his first wedding playing engagement, Adrian Taylor had to provide music for a bride who wore a pink panther outfit, accompanied by the male members of the wedding party dressed as Star Wars stormtroopers.

The payment of organist church fees is often as late as many brides, and has to be extracted from couples in the rush to get photos, hair, frocks and flowers sorted. Robert Bowles was booked to play for one such pair but the vicar warned him that they had been unreliable even when making their preparation. On the day the fees, requested in advance, had not arrived. But then, neither had the bride or the groom. Both vicar and organist doubted the happily dozy couple would materialise at all.

> "The church was empty at the appointed time, but about 20 minutes later people started turning up, and after 30 minutes the bride and bridegroom arrived (together), with the best man and ushers. It was evident that they had all been delayed by being in the pub rather than by traffic problems. The vicar had some serious discussions in the porch, the outcome of which was that he agreed to proceed, provided the fees were paid in cash. But they had no cash — it had all been spent in the pub.
>
> He suggested they either had a whip round among the congregation, or went back to the pub and borrowed what was needed. He observed that the pub must have done very nicely from their party, and since all involved were locals they could surely arrange something. They chose the return-to-pub option, which was ultimately (after about 45 minutes) successful.
>
> This gave me the opportunity to play every piece of music in my music case, and extemporise extensively on *Adeste Fideles* (*Why are we waiting*). But I received only the standard fee."

Edward Peterson had an unexpected fee windfall in the early 1970s when he was Music Director and Organist at St John's Cathedral in Milwaukee, Wisconsin, when the standard fee for a cathedral wedding was $50. A bride wanted her uncle, who had a small home organ, to play for her wedding although it was Edward's responsibility to play at the cathedral. Under cathedral regulations, the uncle had to prove to Edward that he could handle the instrument, but since he would be arriving too late to do a trial run, Edward told the bride she would have to accept the cathedral rulings. The fearsome bride was not to be put off.

> "She told me she hated the way I played the organ, and insisted her uncle be allowed to provide the music."

Edward was taken aback. He told the bride he did not wish to play the organ for anyone who hated the way he played, and to tell her uncle he was welcome to do it instead. Edward would let him into the loft and show him around.

The uncle arrived 15 minutes before the wedding, took one look at the four-manual console and declared he did not know anything about pipe organs and could not possibly handle so large an instrument. He left the loft, gave the bride the news and a moment later Edward heard the rustle of her wedding dress as she raced up the stairs in a panic to his office in the loft. A hot debate ensued: the bride insisting Edward be the organist, and he equally insistent that he would not be the organist for anyone who disliked his music. Finally, Edward capitulated, saying he would play the moment he saw five 100 dollar bills on his desk, or else the organ would remain silent. The shocked bride rustled back down the stairs and miracle of miracles, a gentleman promptly arrived with Edward's stated fee.

Feel like packing some extra excitement into an otherwise mundane ceremony? Try not telling the organist exactly what you want. David Macfarlane arrived with no time to spare for a wedding and did not look through the copy of the wedding booklet that he picked up as he entered the church, assuming he had everything he needed to know already in his diary. His relief at arriving on time vanished when the priest announced a hymn after the initial greetings and statement of purpose.

> "The bride had not thought to talk to the organist about this inclusion when discussing her wedding music. Murphy's law prevailed — I had never seen the words before. The congregation had to wait while I went through the process of counting syllables to determine the meter, then look up the metrical index to find a hymn tune.
>
> Now, you would think a seasoned professional would do this calmly, without batting an eyelid, wouldn't you. Then how come I miscounted the number of syllables?"

Communication problems cause many such chaotic turns at nuptials. Barry Williams was asked to deputise at a church where the wedding services were conducted from a small blue book with all the usual hymns at the back.

"The vicar announced hymn number whatever, and I duly played the same number hymn from the hymn book, instead of the blue book; that is, I played *Praise my soul* to the Goss tune — while they sang *Love Divine*. It fits for the first line." Who disembowelled whom afterwards is not recorded.

Singers at weddings are another potential embarrassment. When did it become fashionable for mothers/aunties/baby-sitter of the bride to warble a tear-choked *Amazing Grace* at a squirming congregation? Even professional singers have accidents. Nina De Sole was playing for a wedding where a guest priest was presiding, and a soloist was to sing for the offertory. Usually they performed only one verse of Schubert's *Ave Maria*, but they realised that the priest was conducting the ceremony a little differently and they needed a second verse. As Nina was about to begin the play-over, the singer looked at Nina in panic. "I don't know the words to the second verse, my score's at home!"

Nina realised her own score showed only the first verse but luckily she knew the words from memory. She reassured the singer that she would tell her the words as the second verse progressed, phrase-by-phrase.

> "We began, and the first verse went like a charm. For the second verse, I whispered the words just before she sang them. She sang: 'Ave Mariiia'; I whispered: 'Mater Dei' and she sang: 'Maaaater Dei'; I whispered: 'Ora pro nobis peccatoribus' She sang: 'Oobis nobis, Booobis, oooooribus...' And she then simply invented a mumbo jumbo that sounded like the things I was trying to tell her.
>
> We were embarrassed. After the ceremony, the priest told us that he was so happy to hear the song and even

complimented her on it. We were blushing with shame of course. I always wondered if he was being sarcastic, or he simply was ignorant, or he was trying to lift up our hearts."

Colin Mitchell got an urgent late-night phone call. It was from a distressed clergyman who told him of a Chilean refugee who had refused on Christian grounds to follow military orders, and was to be deported back to Chile. This was in the days of Pinochet, and the outcome would almost certainly have been his death, torture, or imprisonment. Could Colin act as best man if he and his English girlfriend got married the next morning? Colin agreed, and he turned up at 9.45 am to an empty church. At 9.50 the Rector arrived, then five minutes later, the happy couple, with their baby, which they thrust at Colin. Oh, while he was baby-sitting, could he play the wedding marches and a hymn or two?

Ever obliging and with baby in his left-arm, Colin found a few hymn-books, a couple of Orders of Matrimony and the key to the organ. He went to the organ and gently placed the baby on a few hassocks, but the infant was not happy and let Colin know by screaming.

"I picked the baby up and held her once more in my left-arm, her parents now at the West Door. With right-hand and pedals, and a baby balanced precariously on my left arm, I played through the Lohengrin March and then the first hymn, my arm now getting very tired."

It was time to transmogrify into best man, so transferring the baby to his right arm, Colin took his place beside the groom. At the giving of the ring Colin could not recall which pocket it was in, so the baby parcel was passed to the Rector, until Colin found the ring and swapped it for the child.

"With baby in left arm once more, another hymn, a quick signing of the register with the baby now in my right-arm, and then back to the organ for the Mendelssohn. I went to the reception, which consisted of a bottle

> of cheap bubbly, a few sandwiches and cakes supplied by the Rector's wife, a quick speech from me, (with the baby in my right arm), and finally the departure, as we threw a few grains of rice at the happy couple, handed the baby over, and breathed a sigh of relief. The couple stayed with the Rector, who took great delight in waving the marriage-certificate at the police when they called to deport the refugee."

Occasionally organists are privy to behind-the-scenes machinations at events such as weddings and funerals. James Welch was hired to play for a wedding in Santa Barbara for a man who had left his wife to marry his secretary. A lot of people were at this wedding, but probably most of them were not too happy about the circumstances.

> "While I was playing the recessional music, a friend came up to talk to me at the organ while I was playing. He said, 'Pretty tacky, if you ask me. And the worst part of it was that I had to buy a $25 gift for a $10 friend.' He was a colleague of the groom's. At that moment a young man came up to the organ. I asked him if I could help him, and he said that he was there to pick up the tape recorder behind the organ so the happy couple could relive the ceremony on their honeymoon.
>
> My friend blanched. I had to work fast. I said to the young man, 'Just a minute, I want to make sure the recorder got this last piece of music'. Somehow I backed the tape up and hit the record button again and continued playing for what I hoped was long enough to record over that unfortunate statement. We will never know for sure."

Tales of the horrors awaiting organists deputising at unfamiliar churches deserve their own book, and few players have escaped some sort of disaster dealing with unfamiliar instruments. It may be some consolation that organists of the cathedral and concert ilk can be tripped up. Ian Tracey from Liverpool Cathedral has played organs of one form or another from Land's End to the Planet Zog — and he has a cautionary tale:

> "Some years ago, at his wedding interview in a rather prestigious Cheshire church, my cousin, as a part of the preamble, asked the vicar if his cousin could play; to which the vicar indignantly answered 'Oh no! We are very particular about who plays our organ; it is a real treasure and was once played by the great George Frederick Handel'. After convincing him that the cousin, namely me, did it for a living, the vicar consented (and jovially spoke of selling tickets).
>
> The evening before the wedding, as is customary, the gentlemen of the family went out for traditional celebrations. Several of them could have acquitted themselves quite laudably as accompanist to the ceremony, but I had drawn the short straw. As good organists do, out of habit, on a glorious summer morning, we had arrived at church an hour or so before the service; my headache and effects of dehydration being slightly less severe than the rest.
>
> In the loft, I found, to my horror, that the organ was a five-stop, one manual, with no registration aids of any kind; worse still, and quite catastrophic for the outgoing Widor toccata, there were no pedals. Handel had indeed

played it, and left it pretty much as he found it – as, seemingly in the intervening 300 years, had the church. An overhaul or even a good tuning had clearly been avoided, lest the spell of Mr Handel's visitation be broken.

A quick panic glance down the nave showed me several sleepy family organists, one of whom I was able to inveigle into the loft on the pretext of page-turning. As the service progressed, my second cousin gradually became more conscious and a little more animated. He laughingly asked 'and how, pray, Mr Virtuoso, are you going to manage the Widor? Contemplating growing an extra hand are we?' 'Indeed,' I replied with a satisfied smile, 'Yours!' I have never, in all my life, seen such a smug countenance disappear so instantly. Thus, without the aid of even a single 16 foot, with slightly suspect rhythm and lack of co-ordination at the bottom end (and occasional whispered curses as I got in the way of the pedal part) my cousin and his bride processed out to their Widor. Moral of the tale: always check out the instrument before you say, Yes."

Clergy, choirs and congregation

"The Rector was woken up to find his troublesome organist and two policemen on the doorstep."

Love-hate relationships between clergy and organist have kept many a gossip circuit happy through lean times. Although lay people are often surprised at the state of Civil War that can exist in supposedly Christian surroundings, I am amazed that both factions do not try harder to rub each other out.

During a tempestuous time in the life of Lincoln Cathedral, the Dean announced the anthem in his best liturgical voice: "The anthem this evening is Ave Verum Corpus by William Byrd, one-time organist of this cathedral". Neil Shepherd reports that the organist was heard to mutter, quite audibly, "Poor bastard. . . ." Such comments are usually kept politely behind the music desk, but all it takes is one little slip.

An organist was asked to stand in for a Sunday morning service at a Northampton church. The elderly lay reader, renowned for preaching long sermons, was filling in for the vicar, who was on holiday. The organist planned to end with the Widor toccata and had taken a page turner along with him. After 35 minutes the preacher was still grinding on and the organist turned to the page turner and said "Hasn't the silly old bugger got a home to go to?" He did not know that in order to get the sound of the instrument into the church, microphones were placed over the organ and connected to the PA system. His remarks were clearly heard by the congregation and although they probably agreed with the sentiment, that organist was never asked to play there again.

In the days when Toronto The Good had little to offer in the way of entertainment or dining, a favourite source of musical satisfaction was found at St Mary Magdalene's. Ross Trant says tourists came specially to the city to hear organist Healey Willan. When visitors asked about service times, the rector, Father Crummer, became tired of hearing the question,"Will Dr Willan be there?" For a time the response to this was a testy "Yes! Dr Willan will be here, and so will Jesus Christ." He would then hang up.

Many organists have to muddle along with less-than co-operative clergy. For some years David Bridgeman-Sutton was organist at St Peter's in the Yorkshire Village of Arthington.

> "The vicar, one Christmas Day, refused to let me have the music in advance, so I had to sight read. (His sermons certainly suggested that he himself practised the rule of no preparation) No disaster resulted but his assurance that he thought that 'good organists had to be kept on their toes' did not go down well and I resigned soon after.
>
> A few months later, a young friend of ours in the village succumbed to a lifelong illness and I was asked to play for her (weekday) funeral. This was impossible owing to work commitments; the vicar had to make other arrangements. Shortly after her funeral, a letter arrived from her parents expressing thanks, in the most kindly terms, for the effort I had put in at their daughter's funeral. From some families, it might have been sarcasm but not from that one. We are all used to playing without thanks; this must be a rare example of thanks without playing."

Some seemingly provocative actions can be entirely innocent. A nervous young organ scholar at Cape Town Cathedral once gave the dean the A for the Sursum Corda an octave higher than intended. Over the cathedral microphone system floated the Very Reverend's comment: "What does he think I am, a bloody canary?

It is not all pistols at the pulpit. The organist in a small country parish in the North Island of New Zealand was married to the minister. Her supportive husband, trying to do the right thing, laboriously filled in a long and rather stuffy questionnaire on church music as requested by the Royal School of Church Music. To his credit he solemnly filled it out in detail – until the last question. "Describe your relationship with your organist" it trilled. He thought a lot about that. "I sleep with her" he wrote neatly on the paper, returned it to England. He still wonders if the frisson of excitement the answer caused among the secretaries has subsided.

Everyone uses the phrases *Merry Christmas* and *Happy Easter*, but one of the clergy at Derby Cathedral did not confine his good wishes to the major festivals. The organist, George Handel Heath-Gracie, and members of the choir, would not be surprised if greeted with Merry Michaelmas or Peaceful Pentecost. Michael Whitehall heard how George had his revenge:

> "Before Common Worship arrived on the scene, the Anglican Calendar allocated resounding titles such as Septuagesima to some Sundays, while the feast now coyly referred to as *The Naming of Jesus* had a more direct title. Heath-Gracie was not going to miss the opportunity afforded when 1 January fell on a Sunday — he cheerfully wished the preacher a Merry Circumcision."
>
> "Heath-Gracie had the knack of telling an unlikely story in such a way that it was utterly believable. One of his anecdotes concerned a vicar, anxious to get away early from Evensong. He did not wish to shorten his sermon, so requested the organist to set the psalm to a single, rather than a double chant."

A friend of Frank Fowler was giving a recital when the vicar, who took no interest in the music life of the church and not a lot in any other aspect, had come into the vestry through the back door.

> "Hearing the organ, the vicar wandered over to the console in the chancel, and said to the organist, still playing his recital: 'I need to talk to you about the last hymn on Sunday morning'. The organist simply said 'Bugger off'. The affronted cleric did just that and reported him to the chairman of the Parish Church Council. The PCC were on the organist's side and the chairman asked the cleric if he had realised there was a recital in progress. 'What recital?' was the reply. The organist was congratulated on his self control."

To be fair, vicars are not the only people to blunder across an organist in action. One English organist was press-ganged into buying tickets for the vicar's wine and cheese party by a member of the congregation while he was playing the communion hymn. The compelling sales pitch started with "Are you busy?"

Even fully fledged concerts are no barrier to the determined blunderer, as Hans Hielscher discovered as he was playing an organ recital on a Saturday night. He had just started the first pages of Bach's Fantasia in G minor when the verger went up to the console, tapped him on his shoulder, waved a sheet of paper and shouted against the full organ: "Here are the hymn numbers for the service tomorrow morning." The verger put the paper on the upper manual and disappeared. Hans managed to keep playing, but he had to use that manual soon. He blew on the paper which wafted onto the pedal board.

> "It was not until I had started the fugue that I got one hand free and could remove my Sunday hymns list from the pedal board. After the recital, I tried to teach my verger some basic ideas of the meaning of an organ recital, and the function of the keyboards in particular."

The church where David Aprahamian Liddle plays is used by the Melkites and Maranites, whose liturgy is mostly in Arabic, so confusion is always highly possible.

> "The first time I played for a Melkite wedding, Fr X and I had not sufficiently clarified his verbal signals to me. I had only three slots to play for, so needed three signals. So, at the third 'yes' from Fr X, I launched into the Widor toccata, fondly imagining that the happy couple were processing out; we had all been in church for quite long enough already. I was more than a little perturbed when, after the final crashing cadence of the Widor, I heard yet more Arabic chanting and continued liturgy.
>
> Eventually a lady appeared at the organ console and asked 'Do you think we could have that last piece again now, please?' It was odd to repeat the Widor, and I slunk away afterwards in utter embarrassment. Ever since, I have always done my best to be certain that Fr X and I know our signals."

When Colin Mitchell was about sixteen he played an old organ that had its blower in the rafters of the chancel, and which emitted curious sounds when switched on. Colin was a young anarchist, the vicar was old, and clashes were inevitable.

> "The usual trick was to wait for the words, 'In the name of the Father' as the vicar came to the end of the sermon before announcing the next hymn. I would press the ON button; the blower would burst into life and make a sound that was indistinguishable from the sound of a flushing toilet. I never tired of it."

Blowers are not the only pieces of equipment to provide amusement. One Sunday morning Faythe Freese was playing the organ prelude and heard the amplified sound of a toilet flushing throughout the acoustically resonant sanctuary. "Ah, I thought, the associate pastor forgot to turn off his portable microphone again."

A word of warning: clergy, do not mess with the organist — he is louder than you. An organist arranged to sit with blind Parisian composer and organist Jean Langlais during Mass. Langlais drew some stops and embarked on an impressive improvisation.

> "As the clergy procession started, Langlais wound the improvisation down until it was all shimmering celestes, harmonic flute and Gallic atmosphere. Unfortunately, before Langlais had finished, the voice of the celebrant exhorted the flock to prayer. In an flash of outrage, Langlais kicked the ventils, ended on the chamades and almost destroyed the church. With the sound still reverberating around the building, Langlais turned to the organist beside him and said 'Ziss priest, he is a monster'!"

Occasionally, David Bridgeman-Sutton would fill in for a service, at the request of a vicar who had seven churches.

> "His rule was that in every church there was an organists' book. People who played had to sign in, and received a cheque in due course (£5 for a normal service). Over perhaps a 100 occasions, I signed only once — most parishes were short of money.
>
> "The occasion I did claim was at the only wealthy church in the group. The vicar had included a highly unsuitable hymn tune, one of his own favourites. It was much too high, so I lowered it by a tone (still not suited to village congregations). Half way through the service, the regular organist arrived. She had been sent off to some distant church by the vicar, because she, rightly, had refused to play that tune. It turned out that there was a squabble about the music involving a number of people including the local squire/churchwarden/treasurer. Unwittingly dragged into this, I signed the book —

and still await the cheque 12 years later. The squire was on the other side."

How do you get rid of an organist? F.P.Harton, author of among other tomes, *Elements of Spiritual Life,* wrote a simple letter to Penelope Betjeman, wife of Sir John, the Poet Laureate.

"My dear Penelope,

"I have been thinking over the question of the playing of the harmonium on Sunday evenings here and have reached the conclusion that I must now take it over myself.

I am very grateful to you for doing it for so long and hate to have to ask you to give it up, but, to put it plainly, your playing has got worse and worse and the disaccord between the harmonium and the congregation is becoming destructive of devotion. People are not very sensitive here, but even some of them have begun to complain, and they are not usually given to that. I do not like writing this, but I think you will understand that it is my business to see that divine worship is as perfect as it can be made. Perhaps the crankiness of the instrument has something to do with the trouble, I think it does require a careful and experienced player to deal with it.

Thank you ever so much for stepping so generously into the breach when Sibyl was ill; it was the greatest possible help to me and your results were noticeably better then than now. Yours ever, F.P. Harton" [5]

Sometimes the clergy have every right to despair of their musical staff. Keith John tried the patience of one of his rectors at St Mary de Crypt church in Gloucester:

---

5 John Amis & Michael Rose. Words About Music. London Wiedenfeld & Nicolsons. Citing Bowra, C.M. Memories: 1898-1939

"An incident arose simply because my organ playing and composing took place in the early hours of the morning in the city centre. I was busy composing my first, serious and, of course, 'great' work for organ and I found that I could really concentrate and make progress by cycling the two miles from home to the quiet, deserted church at the dead of night.

After several successful expeditions, I was disturbed one night by a loud knocking on the back door of the church. I ignored it thinking it was just another drunk from the churchyard but the knocking persisted and, eventually, a voice said, 'This is the police'. They thought someone had broken into the church and was mucking about with the organ. So much for my masterpiece of contemporary organ literature.

They also could not believe that this long-haired layabout was organist of the church and a serious musician. Who could verify this? The Rector, of course, and so I was marched down the road to the vicarage whereupon the Rector was woken up to find his troublesome organist and two policemen on the doorstep. He duly identified me and, on our next meeting, reprimanded me but at the same time sympathising with me for wanting to work late into the night."

The power of music to move mountains is almost literally true and some clergy have been wise enough to harness this force if all else fails. When the call girls of Paris held a protest meeting about council regulations in the Church of the Madeleine, their actions triggered a number of sympathetic responses from their sisterhood around the world, even in Australia. It was announced in a Melbourne newspaper that the prostitutes from Melbourne's red light district were planning a similar meeting that morning, and had decided to hold it in St Paul's Cathedral. Director of Music June Nixon thought it might be an interesting morning to catch up on some organ practice.

"Before long, the Dean knocked on the console door to tell me that some women had gathered in the cathedral, and wanted to hold a meeting. He did not want them to hold their meeting in the cathedral, but he did not want to be seen to be throwing them out of the church either. He asked me if I would please play the organ extremely loudly for the next hour or so. I did, and they went away."

Some visitors are much more welcome. Roy Massey, well-known for the use of a bon-mot himself, had a visit from the famous poet John Betjeman one Sunday morning, just before Choral Matins. Sir John asked if he could see the organ.

"In those days Betjeman was well known not only as a poet but also as a television personality, so I was delighted to take him up the very narrow staircase to the organ loft and show him the console. By which time the service was due to begin so he said his farewells and began to negotiate the very narrow stairs once again. He started off by going forwards then changed his mind and tried going backwards, only to lose his nerve and got stuck half way down. At that time of his life Betjeman was a big man and slightly unsteady on his feet, so I did my best to help him and eventually he arrived safely at the bottom. In the meantime, the cathedral choir was processing in total silence as the organ should have been playing.

At the end of the service I went to the clergy vestry to apologise for the fact that the organ had not been playing, but much enjoyed delivering the punch-line of the reason for it — I had had the Poet Laureate stuck on my organ loft stairs."

Being an organist would not be nearly as much fun without the choir. Life would also be a lot easier. Keeping choristers under control and getting them organised is only half the battle; in addition they have to be trained to sing. With as many breeds of chorister as wrong notes, ensuring they all rub along happily together requires considerable skill on the part of the choirmaster.

Church choirs that I have heard range from my rural Kiwi mob that included a heavyweight wrestler, a motorbike gang member, three grandmothers, and a sheepdog (who managed descants quite nicely), through to what appeared to be the retired members of the Paris opera chorus singing (sic) at St Clotilde when we paid a visit. Both choirs challenged the generally accepted definition of Western music, although visually they were charming. Singing quality aside, even the most motley choir can provide support and entertainment for the fugue-fatigued music director.

David Briggs (one of two musicians by that name), now Director of Music at Aldeburgh Parish Church, was a former layclerk at Ely Cathedral, where the choir sang many compositions by Arthur Wills, who was organist at the time. David visited Ely Cathedral for Evensong in the mid 1990s and was astonished to see that the entire service consisted of music by Arthur. Then he spotted Arthur (by then retired) and his wife, Mary, sitting in the stalls opposite.

> "It transpired that the music had been chosen in honour of Arthur's 70th birthday. The anthem was his *The Praises of the Trinity* and, although beautifully sung, I could not help remarking to Arthur afterwards that perhaps it lacked that certain amount of fire that he would have encouraged in our singing in the 1970s. Quick as a flash he retorted, tongue-in-cheek and with a wry smile, 'Well, it will probably be better when they know it'."

Arthur Wills' choir rehearsals were reasonably brief, as he rightly expected layclerks to know the music before coming to rehearsal. He also applied this expectation to his assistant, who was usually note-perfect. However, according to David Briggs, one day the assistant organist was having a few problems with a fiendishly difficult organ pedal passage in a modern anthem.

> "We heard 'Sorry' drifting down from the organ loft much more than was usual. I am told that, between the rehearsal and the service, one of the layclerks placed in the organ loft a 'gift'. The attached note read '*Thought these might help*'. The gift was a pair of skis."

Richard Dawson was playing at a church that had an elderly choir of four ladies and two men. The organ console was opposite the choir, which they had to process past at the end of the service.

> "At the end of the service I started playing a jubilant improvisation in the form of a toccata, with the tune in the pedals. I was dressed in formal attire but was wearing some colourful and patterned socks. After about half a minute the choir started going past, and the last pair to come out were husband and wife. She stopped and said to her husband 'Ooh Ken, look at his socks!' She then pulled up my trouser leg while I was still playing, and pointed them out to him."

Plein Mischief

"I don't know what came over me, but with narrowed eyes, I . . ."

Long hours on unyielding organ benches are partly to blame for organists indulging in mischief-making. The reward for listening closely to those pre-service or outgoing voluntaries might be the revelation that what sounded like a Bach fantasia was in fact a thinly disguised version of *Pop Goes the Weasel?* Next time a bride is more than a few minutes late, see if you can spot a tune such as *Get me to the church on time* peeking through the strands of the organist's improvisation.

Some organists just like to frolic. For several years Michael Koller served as organist at a large church in the Seattle area, and a good friend of his who sang in the choir would often provide challenging musical material to stretch his creative abilities.

> "Often these took the form of a musical dare. I had to exercise great care to hide the melodies being extemporised upon, or risk certain firing, not to mention eternal damnation. The most memorable dare (which I fully incorporated as an ornamented chorale and later as a slow-moving pedal solo under strings) took place on Pentecost Sunday. The theme involved? The rock and roll standard '*Come On Baby, Light My Fire*'."

Brave souls do not attempt to disguise their themes, especially when the antics of in-fighting ecclesiastical powers are enough to push an organist over the figurative edge. John Scott Whiteley was organist at York Minster when David Jenkins was consecrated as Bishop of Durham at York in July 1984.

As he was a man of liberal theological leanings, and something of an academic, the stage was set for a show-down between the then rival factions within the Anglican church: the liberal high churchmen, and the evangelicals. On the day, a posse of assembled protesters gathered to greet the new bishop as he left York Minster by the great west door. A noisy protest took place during the service and a shouting heckler was escorted from the building. It was not quite war, but a scuffle formed as the unfortunate bishop had to run the gauntlet of banners and verbal abuse. What did John Scott Whiteley play as he left? Mendelssohn's *War March of the Priests,* of course.

George Riseley, organist at Bristol Cathedral from 1876-98 found himself in a legal tussle with the Dean and Chapter. It is said that the case, having gone to court, was won by the organist, who returned to the cathedral, choosing for the voluntary after Evensong *Fixed in his everlasting seat* from Handel's *Semele*.

Katherine Dienes-Williams' irrepressible sense of fun has been responsible for the strains of *Puff the Magic Dragon*, themes from Eastenders, Coronation Street, Match of the Day, Neighbours, Home and Away; *Jingle Bells, Happy Birthday* or other incidental tunes being heard during divine worship.

An organ is fair game for pranksters. An issue of *The Organ* magazine in the late 1940s noted that James Kendrick Pyne, organist of Manchester Cathedral from 1876 to 1908, had a flair for mechanical contrivances. He designed a mechanism that would automatically turn on the blower (probably a hydraulic one) as soon as someone sat on the organ bench, and turn it off when the seat was vacated. One of his choirboys, also of practical bent, one day reversed the levers, so that the blower was normally on but was turned off when someone sat on the bench. The reservoirs of the instrument were large and James was well launched into an incoming voluntary when the supply ran out, with the usual wailing noises.

As a young Royal College of Music student, David Harrison arrived at Southwark Cathedral for a special service for clergy, and was invited by Sidney Campbell to join him at the organ. David sat, unsuspecting, on the stool to the right of Sidney as he accompanied the opening hymn. At the end of the first verse, Sidney turned to David and barked "your turn", getting off the stool as he said it.

> "I had to gather my thoughts while wriggling into position for verse two, which somehow I managed. Having got my breath back I set to work to plough through this hymn on a large cathedral organ which I had not played before, accompanying a large and vocal collection of clergy. How I managed I do not know, but by verse three I was playing with a more or less straight bat. Sidney then opened the doors behind me which look into the choir stalls, leaned over the edge and grinned happily at the assembled parsons. He soon got bored with this and found all the gowns, cassocks, surplices and hoods in the organ loft, and draped them over my shoulders as I struggled to play."

The incorrigible Roy Tankersley should not be let loose anywhere near an organ during a recital. So it was with some trepidation that Martin Setchell warily agreed to Roy's request to play for a civic organ concert in the town hall in Dunedin, New Zealand. The organ was the beloved Hill, Norman and Beard Romantic behemoth, affectionately known as Norma. As Martin was playing, a sheet of paper appeared through the gap between the top manual and the wood, straight into the path of Martin's galloping fingers. 'Boo!' written on it in large cheeky letters, was testimony to Roy's presence among Norma's innards, safe from retaliation.

When adolescent pipe organ fanatics Tim Bell and his friend Pierre were students at Nelson College in New Zealand, they found a way to get among the pipes. Pierre had figured out the configuration of the relays for the electric action, and was able to play tunes by over-riding them.

> "I was practising at the console one morning, while Pierre was adding a descant part on tromba from within the bowels of the organ. This went well until the music master dropped in to talk to me. My three-handed playing may have sounded impressive, but the master's face rapidly turned to confusion when I stopped playing and the descant continued. The topic was changed quickly, and I never knew if he found out what was happening."

Tim was one of the organists for the morning assembly singing at Nelson College. He had some friends, clearly bursting with kiwi inventiveness, who were (a) very keen on electronics and (b) were dying to pull a prank during assembly.

> "One morning I arrived to find a spurious wire heading out of the organ console, and found that it connected a switch in the audience to both a piston and note on the console, so that my friends could operate it at their leisure while the headmaster was speaking. Another time I arrived to find an old headlamp behind the organ. Again, I managed to foil the plot by tracing the setup. The headlamp was a parabolic reflector for a light-sensitive transistor that again triggered the piston and a note, this time by shining a torch from the gallery onto the headlamp — remote control 1970s style."

The ever-humble harmonium is an excellent target for vandalism. As timid 10 year-olds at boarding school we idolised those wags who had passed into school folk lore many years earlier by filling the empty cavities of the harmonium with tennis balls. The resultant bongo drum effect during chapel was guaranteed to set elderly mistresses' pince-nez vibrating and coiffure unravelling. When the school eventually invested in a pipe organ it gained twofold; it put a stop to this un-ladylike pastime and the school gained a superior instrument.

Elsewhere in New Zealand, myriad opportunities for torturing clergy offer themselves to the creative player. In the 1970s the Monday evening services in Dunedin's Knox Theological College chapel were always taken by a student, and no staff were present. The organist decided a particularly earnest theological student needed to 'lighten up'. After the unsuspecting officiating student had taken his place in the chancel the organist began to bring the voluntary to a close. Sensing an ending, the student stood to start the service, at which point the organist carried on playing. The student sat down. The organist again moved into a rallentando, heralding a classic perfect cadence. The student stood. The organist neatly turned it into an interrupted cadence and cheerfully continued. The student returned to his seat. Another diminuendo and gentle ritardando signalled the end was near, so the student got to his feet once more. The organist blithely played on. After five such yo-yo attempts to begin the service, the student leaned forward and spoke loudly into the microphone, "Let us worship God!" The members of the congregation were by now helpless with mirth and clutched each other in quaking heaps in the pews, quite unready for worship.

Simple revenge comes in handy. When at school in England, a young lad I will call Fred spent his days in abject misery. He was barely able to contain his delight when, at 15, he fled the school forever. The headmaster was a sadistic and odious character, but a pillar of society and lay-reader when he was not swishing a cane and terrorising small boys.

> "The boys of the school had variously and unsuccessfully plotted the demise of the headmaster, the destruction of the school, or some sort of mass-escape undetected. We had left gas-taps turned on in the Chemistry Lab, put phenolphaline in the headmaster's cup of tea, swapped the labels on the gas-jars in the hope that he would end up with trench-gas syndrome; we were noth-

ing but failed assassins and arsonists. The scars of boyhood had largely healed by the time I was 22, but one Sunday, I recoiled in horror upon entering church to play the organ, to see my former headmaster there as the officiant at Evensong."

The headmaster had a magnificent singing voice, and never missed the chance to show it off. Every sung item, even the responses, became solos with background choral accompaniment. Fred felt revenge coming on.

> "I do not know what came over me, but with narrowed eyes, I gently pushed in the Choir Dulciana and drew instead, the five-rank Harmonics (15,17,19, b21 and 22). I pressed bottom G for the response note, following which there was a moment of hesitation and a look of real panic on the face of the headmaster. To my utter delight, he pitched it wrong, tried to correct himself, and ended up singing 'O lord open thou our lips' to a wonderful arpeggio of the dominant 7th, the choir responding with the tonic."

Benchmarks

"... the organ company later returned those parts of my pants which stuck on the bench and which they had to scrape off."

Organ seats frequently afford the player an aerial view of goings-on below. Although some areas around the organ console are so spacious an orchestra can be easily accommodated, others have barely enough room to swing a page turner. But the best thing about a loft is that the territory is the organist's domain. For the beleaguered musician it is an inner sanctum, and the secrets lying there can be delicious indeed. So what goes on up there? You would be surprised.

According to David Harrison, Guillaume Ormond (organist of Truro Cathedral from 1929 to 1970) was seen indulging in some cooking.

> "The detached console did not appear until 1963 and so Ormond was marooned upstairs for much of his tenure. It was possible to view some parts of the organ loft from the choir stalls and the dean was surprised, one day, to glance idly upwards during one of the spoken parts of the service and spot bacon and eggs being fried on the organist's bench."

It is also alleged that Ormond had a typewriter in the loft that he used during sermons. He was not a fast typist and those not in the know feared death watch beetle had got into the organ.

An organist visiting Westminster Abbey asked one of Andrew Lumsden's predecessors, Osborne Peasgood, if he could sit in the loft during a service, which he duly did. He sat where he could see a lot of the console but not the music desk. At the end of the service, Peasgood played a Bach Prelude and Fugue. The organist was quite an aficionado of editions, but saw Peasgood turn the pages in places that made him wonder which edition he was using. After the piece had finished, he walked across to the console to discover that Peasgood had been reading a motorcycle magazine.

On his first visit to Notre Dame de Paris with his choir, Neil Shepherd sat at the side of the orgue de choeur (being played that day by Yves Castagnet). At one point, the organist accompanied the psalm with one hand and feet, while having a telephone conversation with the titulaire on duty in the tribune.

> "On my second visit there, the same organist, again, while accompanying the psalm with one hand, was sending text messages with the other. Entertaining to say the least."

The loft in Notre Dame de Paris enjoys a vibrant social life, in fact. In the 1990s, from alongside the console, Martin Setchell and I were mesmerised by Olivier Latry's extemporisations. Olivier had used the big reeds in various ways, and we were reeling from the effects of being just beneath the trumpets en chamade. But something was not quite right. Olivier kept looking around and we too thought we could hear something: was it a loose pipe? A faint knocking that had not been audible over roaring reeds and screaming mixtures came through in a fleeting pianissimo moment. Olivier leapt from his stool and opened a small door in the organ case behind him. From inside the case shot a technician who had been accidentally locked in before the start of the service. He reeled his way, cross-eyed and hair standing on end, towards the loft exit.

The position and height of the stool is critical, and users who fiddle with a set height are reserved special places in the fires of Hell. James Lancelot's senior organ scholar at King's College, Cambridge, was taller than James, and he started the Giant Fugue after Evensong one day before realising that the stool was at the wrong height. James and the organ scholar moved like the wind.

> "I cancelled the pedal stops; he stood up; I frantically inserted the blocks under the stool; he sat down; I restored the pedal stops; in came the first pedal entry, with about a quaver to spare. We would not have dared let it turn out any other way."

Perfectly positioned items can be subtly changed between rehearsal and concert, particularly the height of the bench or the distance between it and the console. The alteration can be innocently made by an organ tuner or someone slipping in to practice. A relocated bench once had Christopher Herrick hanging on for dear life during the tricky pedal passages in Bach's Prelude and Fugue in A minor. "Now I always make sure of my bench height and position by placing small sticky dots strategically. These dots are often still in place when I make a return appearance years later."

The Dutch organist Gerard Bunk, who found his bench to be quite literally a sticking point, related this tale in his biography[6]:

> "I had been invited to play for a re-inauguration recital at a recently-restored organ. For this occasion, they had not only restored the instrument but also painted and varnished the console and the organ bench. During the afternoon of the recital day, I had practised the organ for several hours before a choir arrived that I had to accompany and rehearse with, until a few minutes before the recital. So, I decided to stay on the organ bench all the time until the beginning of the recital.

6 *Bunk. Liebe zur Orgel*, Erinnerungen aus Einem Musikerleben

But at the end of the recital when I finally wanted to descend from the organ bench, it turned out to be impossible, because I was firmly connected to it and I had not realised it before. So, I had to wait until the choir had left the organ gallery. I do not dare to describe in which turn-out I left the organ bench. The only thing I can add here is that the organ company later returned those parts of my pants which stuck on the bench and which they had to scrape off."

Organists at large

Characters

"Just because I wrote it does not mean that I can play it."

Being something of a character, if not downright eccentric, appears to go with the job. Gerald Gifford researched tales of the more well-known figures in English musical history and discovered among them an intriguing 18th century individual in Gloucester by the name of Jeffries: [7]

> "He would appear to have led a colourful life, and we can only begin to imagine the tact with which he would probably have conducted himself in the Cathedral Close. Sir John Hawkins takes up the story:
>
> 'Stephen Jeffries, a pupil of Michael Wise, in 1680, being then but twenty years of age, was elected organist of Gloucester Cathedral, which office he held thirty four years. . . . The choirmen of Gloucester relate that, to

7 Sir John Hawkins: History of the Science and Practice of Music, London 1776. Quoted by Gerald Gifford in article in the Organist's Review, 2004/2 Vol xc No 354, 130-131

cure him of a habit of staying late at the tavern, his wife drest up a fellow in a winding-sheet, with directions to meet him with a lanthorn and candle in the cloisters through which he was to pass on his way home; but that, on attempting to terrify him, Jeffries expressed his wonder only by saying, 'I thought all you spirits had been abed before this time'.

Hawkins continues with another tale:

> 'That Jeffries was a man of singular character we have another proof in the following story related of him. A singer from a distant church, with a good voice, had been requested and undertook to sing a solo anthem in Gloucester Cathedral, and for that purpose took his station at the elbow of the organist in the organ loft. Jeffries, who found him trip in performance, instead of palliating his mistake and setting him right, immediately rose from his seat, and leaning over the gallery, called out aloud to the choir and the whole congregation, 'He can't sing it.'

Organists often have to work alongside other musicians. In the late 1960s, an amateur choral society in Birmingham gave a rare performance of Liszt's *Via Crucis*, *Meditations on the Fourteen Stations of the Cross*, for chorus and organ. David Sadler heard a spot of quick-thinking repartee from organist Roy Massey, who was then organist at Birmingham Cathedral.

> "At the afternoon rehearsal the conductor would insist that the meditations for solo organ be played in their entirety, leading to a certain amount of restiveness, especially among those singers who were there as unpaid stiffeners of weaker sections such as the tenors, had no connections with the choir, and so felt that valuable time was being wasted. Roy fairly quickly became sensitive to this and managed to deal a suitable death blow:

> Conductor, jovially: "Now Roy, just give us station five (or whatever), if you would not mind."
>
> Roy Massey, straight-faced: "Sorry Jeremy, Dr Beeching closed this one a year or two back!" [8]

Ena Baga, star of the cinema organ for more than 80 years, died in 2004 aged 98. In 1992 she was taken by Bob Heard and his wife, as a surprise, to Thomas Trotter's lunchtime concert in Birmingham Town Hall. Trotter, a great lover of the theatre organ, offered to announce the great player's presence and play her *Bagatelle* piece as an encore. Bob let publisher Stainer and Bell in on the secret and a complimentary copy of the music was sent to Thomas. At the end of the concert, Thomas announced her celebrated presence, an already excited Ena became ecstatic, standing up and bowing from the balcony in full royal mode to a noisy audience below.

> "When Thomas began her *Bagatelle*, Ena became nearly unmanageable — it was wonderful. Afterwards at coffee/lager-time downstairs a little group of us sat with Thomas while a steady stream of 'mature' men filed over to pay their respects — to Ena."

It was only then that Bob realised why so many men were paying attention to her.

> "During the war Ena spent the years deputising for Reginald Dixon at the Tower Ballroom, Blackpool; these men had been stationed at a nearby RAF base and spent a lot of time dancing to Ena's playing. They were regulars at Trotter's lunchtime concerts but on this occasion, Ena was the star attraction."

Healey Willan, not too long before his retirement and death, and well into his 80s, gave a recital at the University of Toronto. Ross Trant was present.

---

8 The Beeching Report axed many of Britain's rail branch lines and small stations in the mid-1960s]

"As always he played brilliantly, and it was a delight and an honour as a student to be there. After the recital he got a standing ovation, much less common in those days than today. As usual, he asked the audience what they would like to hear as an encore. There were immediate requests for his *Introduction, Passacaglia and Fugue*. Dr Willan declined, and suggested something else. The requests for his masterpiece were repeated. Finally, Willan grinned and silenced the demands by saying: 'Just because I wrote it does not mean that I can play it'."

Willan was a Canadian citizen, but at a conference for church musicians and choristers, he described himself as 'Irish by heritage, English by birth, Canadian by adoption, and Scotch by absorption.'

Renowned American TV journalist Walter Cronkite had enjoyed a long and hugely successful career in broadcasting, covering the Vietnam War, the Kennedy assassination, Watergate, and the landing of Apollo 11 on the moon among many other significant events. In 2004 he visited the Mormon Tabernacle to record a narration for a documentary commemorating the Tabernacle Choir's 75 years of broadcasting: *Music and the Spoken Word*. Richard Elliott was asked to demonstrate the Tabernacle organ for him and his entourage during a lull in his schedule. After introducing himself to the 88-year-old Cronkite, Richard asked if he had a request.

"Pardon me?" he replied.

"I asked if you would like to request a particular piece of music," Richard repeated. Cronkite thought for a moment.

"Can you play the *Battle Hymn of the Republic*?" Richard did not have the music at hand for the choir's Grammy-award-winning arrangement, but he had played it enough times that he figured he could pull off an impromptu arrangement for solo organ.

"There ensued what I thought was a very workmanlike, spur-of-the-moment interpretation of the choir and orchestra parts, complete with numerous stop changes, all done without the aid of pistons or a printed score. I slid off the bench to the group's applause and I asked Mr Cronkite if he would like to hear something else."

"Pardon me?" he said.

"I asked if you would like to hear something else." Cronkite paused.

"Can you play the *Battle Hymn of the Republic*?"

Richard was philosophical, oscillating between enforced humility and rationalising that organ music does not come across very clearly through hearing aids.

A playful assortment of characters appeared in an extraordinary sell-out Royal College of Organists centenary concert organised by Peter Hurford at the Royal Albert Hall in September 1966, called *Organ in Sanity and Madness*. Peter dressed as the Queen of Sheba was carried in an open Palanquin by six Choral Scholars from King's College Chapel Choir (some of whom were later to form the King's Singers) to the appropriate music by Handel. Many cathedral organists joined in, and several pieces were specially written for the occasion, such as a mini-concerto for 484 penny whistles by John McCabe, conducted by David Willcocks. The whistles were on sale to the audience at the door and David rehearsed the audience during the concert before performing it with orchestra. He also conducted variations on the nursery rhyme *Humpty Dumpty* written by Gordon Jacob, with actions required from the audience (also rehearsed during the concert). Alan Wicks entered wearing a dressing gown which he removed to reveal boxing shorts beneath, and then played *Il Combattimento d'Organo e Batteria (percussion)* by Alan Ridout, with James Blades as percussionist.

When the composer can help with interpretation of his or her music, it pays to take heed. Marie-Louise Jaquet-Langlais, a former pupil and the widow of Jean Langlais, tells of the time he was composing his *Poemes Evangeliques* in 1932. Langlais wanted to recreate the atmosphere of the scene where the Christ was received with enthusiasm by the crowd in *Les Rameaux*. He indicated this in the score, with tutti, very fast and legato, with the Gregorian theme *Hosanna Filio David* appearing in the pedal, loudly and majestically. Before Palm Sunday in 1935, Langlais met Messiaen, who told him he was going to play *Les Rameaux* at La Trinité church but also told Langlais not to go. Of course, Langlais went. He could not believe what he heard.

> "The piece was played by Messiaen very slowly, everything staccato, and with a pedal so soft that you could not hear the Gregorian theme on the pedal. I came back home and wrote Messiaen the following note: 'I heard my *Rameaux* this morning at La Trinité. If you are still a good friend of mine, do not play again one note of my music, please'."

Langlais waited for an answer, which never came. So he phoned Messiaen. "Did you receive my letter ?" "Yes." "What did you think about it?" "I thought it very funny, but, come next year at La Trinité and I will play your work again."

The next year Langlais went to the church and heard the most magnificent interpretation of his *Rameaux* he had ever heard. "Nobody has ever played it in this way after him! That was Messiaen!" (Ironically Jean Langlais complained during a master class late in his career: "The trouble with you English is that you want to play ALL the notes.")

The legendary Sidney Campbell, organist of St George's Chapel, Windsor, was a heavy smoker, remembers Jason Smart.

> "It was quite usual to see him light up to walk the 50 yards from his house to the chapel for Evensong. He smoked Senior Service — high tar, untipped and possibly the most lethal cigarette on the market.

At one Evensong we were chatting in the interval between the Nunc Dimittis and the anthem while down below the choir sang the Creed and the responses. Campbell had swung his legs over the organ bench and was sitting facing me with his back to the console. As we chatted I saw him reach into his pocket and pull out his cigarette packet. My eyes widened as he nonchalantly extracted a cigarette and began tapping one end on the packet to compress the tobacco, talking all the while. Then, as if unaware of what he was doing, he casually put the cigarette in his mouth and brought out his lighter. Horrified, I hissed urgently, 'You can't smoke that in here!' — at which Campbell dissolved into silent laughter. I had been well and truly 'had'. Two weeks later he tried the same trick again. This time I offered him a light."

Eric Thiman realised the importance of visiting organist associations trying the City Temple organ if only to be able to say to their grandchildren that they had once played the instrument. He and Frank Fowler would move to the back of the church to listen.

"Some of the players could be excellent and pleased him; others evoked such asides as 'Well, at least it was not Crimond with the tremulant on'. After a very dodgy performance of one of his own pieces he turned to me and said, 'You know, I think that I could almost have written something like that'."

Across the Channel, French organists battled similar unfamiliarity with the instrument. Charles Tournemire, titular organist at Sainte-Clotilde in Paris, France, was regularly invited to participate in musical salons. Frank Mento says that during these occasions he would play brilliant improvisations on the piano. The people who attended these gatherings were far from musical connoisseurs. A lady went up to the composer and asked, "Maestro, what are the black keys and white keys used for?" In his kindly fashion, Charles said, “The black keys are for funerals and the white keys are for weddings.”

People would flock to hear Charles Tournemire improvise since he was extremely imaginative and would improvise as he felt. One day, at the end of Mass he improvised softly on strings. Someone came up to him and said, “Maestro, it’s time to play the Recessional. People are going out of church.” Tournemire replied, “Well, go out!”

Edward Elgar was conducting a rehearsal of the Dream of Gerontius in the Royal Albert Hall. When it came to *Praise to the Holiest* he stopped the performers after a few moments and asked the organist to ‘make more noise’. They started again. Once more, Elgar stopped proceedings after a few moments and asked ‘Mr Organist’ to ‘make more noise’. Off they went for the third time, only to be stopped again. “Mr Organist, do you have a Tuba on that thing?” “Yes maestro, several.” “Good — use them all!”[9]

Benefactors of organs come in all shapes, sizes and wallets. Fred Swann often played the evening service and recital at the Fourth Presbyterian Church of Chicago when he was a student at Northwestern University in the 1950s. One evening an elderly lady waited for him to come down from the organ loft, and she introduced herself as the daughter of the donor of the Skinner organ. She recalled how, as a young girl, she walked down the aisle of the church with her mother and Ernest M. Skinner, whom she had chosen to build the organ for the new church. She told Fred:

> “As they arrived at the front of the church my mother gestured to the large, empty organ chamber above and said to Mr Skinner: ‘There is the hole. Fill it up and send me the bill’.”

9 John Maslen adds that this story was noted down by the man who later conducted the Goldsmiths' Choral Union in the 1960s, and who was at that time a student, and whose own copy of the ‘Dream’ was duly annotated ‘With Tubas’.)

Perhaps the oddest experience Christopher Herrick had at Westminster Abbey came after the rehearsal for William Walton's funeral service. He was instructed to play a snippet of Walton's film music 'as loudly as possible' at the end of Laurence Olivier's declamation of Henry V's Agincourt speech from the abbey pulpit. Lord Olivier built up a rhetorical climax in his inimitable manner:

"And gentlemen in England, now abed
Shall think themselves accurs'd they were not here,
And hold their manhoods cheap whiles any speaks
That fought with us upon Saint Crispin's daaaay."

"Following my brief, I roared in with full organ as he in turn sustained the last word at full throttle. Afterwards, an urgent message came via the Dean's verger that Lord Olivier wanted to see me. Help! Although what transpired might be commonplace in theatrical circles, there cannot be many organists who are able to boast that the all-time great actor of stage and screen, Laurence Olivier, has thrown his arms round him in a big embrace and said: 'What an honour it was to work with you'!"

Without a bench back or handrail, nothing stops the organist from plummeting to the pews below

Living dangerously

Real blood has been frequently spilled in the line of organ duty, and dark smears found on the odd organ console testify to it.

To a layman, an organist is a spinster Aunty Hazel who smells of horse liniment, pumping out *The Old Rugged Cross* on a harmonium; hardly one to espouse a risky career. Not so. The work of an organist, whether it be in a cathedral, concert hall or chapel, has dodgy, and sometimes downright scary, moments.

Minor earthquakes in New Zealand are a common enough congregation-awakening annoyance; but sometimes the 'quakes are substantial and not well-timed. I was playing for a wedding in Christchurch, and the couple had just started to sign the register, when a whopper 'quake — more than six on the Richter scale — surged its way through the province. The nave lights swayed, the wedding party wobbled, and the congregation clutched their bosoms in fear. Set on a wooden floor, the organ console jerked away to my left. Mildly wondering what I should do as the congregation dived under the pews, I automatically played on, but with my hands still in the same position over the keys that had whipped about five notes left.

"Uh-oh, that's not right." I moved my fingers en masse to the left also and kept playing. At which point the rolling of the quake thrust the console to the right, but with my brain semi-paralysed, I stuck where I was, doggedly playing down a fifth.

"Er, that's not right either." So back up I trundled to find where the keys had got to. For the next 15 seconds or so I played tag with the keyboard, transposing willy-nilly, and resulting in the most exotic harmonies to have ever been associated with early English dances. Twenty minutes later the lights were still swaying and my fingers still shaking. Of a more practical nature, Katherine Dienes-Williams was seen bolting for the exit when an earthquake struck during a service she was playing for the medical profession in Wellington Cathedral.

> "As I began to play the Herbert Howells voluntary at the gallery balcony console, I thought I was getting very emotionally involved as I seemed to be swaying to and fro — only to hear shortly thereafter the dean shout 'get to the sides' as the procession was walking out and a 6.5 earthquake rolled through the building. Well, hang the voluntary, I was out of that console space quick-smart."

Natural disasters are less of a problem than man-made ones. When Jennifer Bate played in Jamaica in 1978, the country was in political turmoil. The streets around Scots Kirk in Kingston were heavily policed, and there was an armed sergeant, in full tropical uniform, standing inside to guard the concert-goers.

> "I played my final piece (Garth Edmundson's Toccata on *Vom Himmel hoch)* and the packed audience applauded. Then, the officer strode down the middle aisle and spoke to the organisers. The applause gave way to a hush, for the audience feared this meant trouble. Anxiously, the organisers came to tell me that the sergeant wanted the last piece again. I explained to the audience, and duly played it. I have returned to Jamaica nine times since, but always on the understanding that the policeman's piece will be the first encore."

In the late 1980s churches in Germany were safe havens for criminals, and therefore not always the best places for organists. American Faythe Freese was living and studying at that time as a Fulbright student in Kiel, in former West Germany. Faythe diligently practised Max Reger's Op. 73 *Original Thema für die Orgel* at Sankte Nikolaikirche daily. Early one morning she was met at the front door by the pastor who told her that the Red Faction, a Neo-Nazi terrorist group, had taken over the church as a place of asylum the evening before, and she would have to return later to practise. When she came back they were still holed-up in the church, so Pastor Kretschmar led her up the back stairwell to the organ console in the balcony.

"Play softly," he whispered and quickly left, locking the balcony door behind him. Faythe sat nervously at the console. Turning slightly she could see the terrorists below, waking from sleep, moving groggily about in various states of undress. Hung high on the walls were white bed sheets upon which had been painted the message, "Release our comrades from the isolation camps!" Faythe expected to be shot in the back as she resolutely practised Op. 73. Every half hour, Pastor Kretschmar would return, instructing her to play a little bit louder.

They might have all been there still had it not been for the moving effects of Herr Reger. After several hours, the terrorists left the church. An article about this episode appeared in the local newspaper, the *Kieler Nachtrichten*, and it ended with a quote from the terrorists speculating that the American organist Faythe Freese was brought in to force them to leave the church by playing Max Reger's music.

Both Cherry Rhodes and Hans Hielscher have literally played their way through revolutions in Europe. In 1968, during her student days in Paris, Cherry was invited to give an organ tour in what was then Czechoslovakia.

> "During the middle of the tour, the Spring Revolution broke out, and I was told that the Russians had come to the border with their tanks. Everybody was in turmoil

> about it. Later the tanks rolled into Prague, followed by the crack-down on dissidents. I was so intent and naïve that I thought, 'Well, I have an organ tour to finish.' And so, I just went about my business as I was trained to do and completed the tour."

Later, on a train to Vienna, Cherry met an American woman who said she had called the Government in Washington, D.C. and had been told it could not be responsible for her safety.

> "Suddenly I could not wait to get out of Czechoslovakia. I became progressively more nervous and frightened, realising that there were two checkpoints to clear between us and the free world. I wondered, 'Are they going to detain us? If they do, our Government is not going to help us! What then?' Twice, armed border guards searched our luggage and interrogated every passenger. I can still see their stern faces. It seemed to take forever. Finally, they waved the train through. What a relief!"

Hans Hielscher played a recital on the Cavaillé-Coll organ in the historic Basilica Santa Maria del Coro in San Sebastian, North Spain, which is part of the Basque region seeking independence from Spain.

> "Unfortunately, these endeavours have not always been peaceful, especially because of the deadly activities of the ETA. The ETA (Euskadi Ta Askatasuna: Basque for 'Basque Homeland and Freedom') is a terrorist organisation, but considered by itself as a paramilitary Basque nationalist armed group demanding Basque independence. They are still active.
>
> I had been warned by the church's priests that they expected ETA activities in downtown San Sebastian, where the basilica was located, later that evening, but that we still should have the recital. So, that afternoon I stayed in the church until the recital to avoid walking in

the street. As expected, when I began my programme at 9 pm there were merely some 30 in the audience. I played as usual, but always aware of shooting that seemed to be close to the church. It was audible even during loud passages of the music.

"After I had finished my programme, we were asked by the priests not to leave the church but stay inside, and they locked all doors as a precaution. So we sat and chatted for another hour, still hearing gunfire in the distance. Eventually, one of the priests called for a taxi and I was guided to a back door of the Basilica, pushed in the taxi, and sent off to my hotel. To be honest, I was somewhat relieved when I left the city alive the next morning."

A world away, Rick Taft arrived in Vietnam in 1968. He recalls a Kafkaesque place, where a tiny oasis of cool existed amid the madness. He stayed at his first stop, the 'repo depot' (where new replacements coming from the States waited to be assigned to a unit), because they needed a supply clerk, and he had eight months stateside experience.

"I was elated. I had already seen the soft-serve ice cream stand. I figured since there were thousands of unarmed transient soldiers there it had to be a relatively safe place. Then I found out that the guy I replaced was one of five casualties in a rocket attack four days before. The first local I met, my housekeeper ('Mama san'), turned out to be the spy who supplied the coordinates for the rocket attack. The first American I met was a wannabe Milo Minderbinder being shipped back to Texas to face bigamy charges.

One day I walked past the chapel and the sign out front said 'Organist Wanted'. The job paid enough for cigarettes and beer. Amazingly, the organ was a Ham-

> mond B-3 with a big Leslie speaker. Wow! I still wonder how such an iconic jazz instrument could have ended up so far from the clubs where it belonged. For the entire time I played there, no more than a handful of people ever showed up for a service. I hope it was not my playing. I also hope that organ was eventually 'liberated' by some private enterprise type who knew what it was, and where it belonged."

Real blood has been frequently spilled in the line of organ duty, and dark smears found on the odd organ console testify to it. These smudges are, however, more likely to be the result of organists impaling themselves on protruding widgets, wodgets and to paper cuts from lightning page turns rather than through fisticuffs caused by degenerated clergy-organist relationships.

In Treviso, Douglas Lawrence was flaying his way through a physically demanding piece by Ron Nagorcka; every limb, digit, and parts of body that can find a space on the console were brought into play for the denouement. As Douglas locked himself in mortal combat with this extravaganza the blood started pouring from his previously cut index finger. The audience were startled during the interval when the priest, approaching the organ console in the sanctuary and in full view of them, saw the blood-stained keys, leapt in the air and screamed "Sangue! Sangue!"

Christopher Herrick had prepared his registrations before a concert on a small organ in Norway. On the day of the concert he needed to tune one of the two reeds that the organ boasted.

> "One was in the Brustwerk so it was quite easy to manage at the console. The main trumpet stop was at the back of the organ, but I needed some extra light for the task. Unfortunately, I couldn't find a switch anywhere, so I tuned it in the dark more or less by feel, pulling down the trackers. One of the pipes resisted change and too strong a tap on the tuning spring sent it flying free of the reed.

> To mend this, I carried it carefully to the console where there was light. Unfortunately, as I returned to the back of the organ, concentrating hard on the valuable restored pipe in my hands, I thwacked the top of my head on some overhead woodwork. To cut a long bloody story short, I came back about one and a half hours later to give the concert with two stitches in my head. It was only after the whole thing was over — flowers, speeches etc — that back in the vestry I happened to notice in a mirror the two trails of dried blood streaking all the way down my face."

Not one person had commented on the fact that they had just enjoyed a concert by the world's most musical Frankenstein's monster.

Climbing up to some organ lofts requires bravery normally expected of mountaineers and child-minders. Julian Cooper still gets clammy hands five years after visiting the organ loft of Toulouse Cathedral in France. Access begins routinely enough by steps up a long spiral stone staircase; then another doorway leads on to a metal walkway in the open air among the flying buttresses. This is still quite safe, but when re-entering the cathedral the visitor is by now very high up and probably suffering from shaking knees. With a stone wall on one side and a 24 metre drop to the ground level on the other, a single metal handrail is the only thing stopping the wobbly knees taking one over the edge. This walkway is about a metre wide with uneven stone, so it is easy to trip. Worse follows.

> "To get to the console, you have to walk along this stone walkway, at which point there is an 24 metre drop on both sides, still with only a single metal handrail on each side for support. Then you go through an archway, down a couple of steps and into the organ console. This feels safer than the route getting there, although the side of the console is only waist-height, and it would easily be possible to tumble over the edge. At this great height, everybody below looks so small and tiny.

> My friend explained to me that he took me to the organ before looking round the cathedral otherwise I might have been put off had I seen the way to get there."

Vertigo-prone organists had to approach the gallery chamber organ in the Basilica of the Blessed Sacrament in Christchurch, New Zealand, with a great deal of caution, crampons, and a large safety net. The only way to play the 1870 Bevington was to line it parallel with the edge of the gallery, and thrust the gullible player onto the parapet before they had a chance to escape. Without a bench back or handrail, nothing stopped the organist from plummeting to the pews below (apart from the thought that it might have made the clergy hallelujahs more heartfelt). A cushion was put on the parapet in deference to a quaint belief in the haemorrhoid-causing properties of concrete, but apart from that, it was the musician versus mechanism and gravity. One vertigo-afflicted organist had the vapours as he dribbled, wild-eyed, out on to the edge. His hands had to be prised from where they clutched the ends of the manuals before he could be persuaded to do what he was there for. Another visiting Australian organist was so emotionally overcome he spent vital pre-concert moments urgently negotiating a few deals with his Maker in a nearby chapel.

Strangely enough, for demigods who can control mighty consoles with every movable limb and digit a human possesses, off-duty organists have been known to be appalling drivers. The sight of one New Zealand cathedral organist's little blue Mini was enough to scatter wise choristers into the bushes. Sean Tucker had the terrifying experience of being given a lift around Caen at night by the titulaire of l'Abbaye aux Hommes.

> "Apart from bumper-pushing some really quite nice shiny cars in order to get out of a parking space, he stopped only once at a red light or a junction. Even then, this was only because he noticed the police car which was about to bisect our path, at the last second. I cannot say that I enjoyed suddenly having my face pressed up against the windscreen while simultaneously being hit

> from behind by a box of tissues, a large hard-back copy of a Victor Hugo novel (*Le Dernier Jour d'un Condamné*) and a bag of courgettes, as Alain stood on the brake pedal and created a skid-mark about 12 feet long, which stank of burnt rubber."

The experience inspired Sean to some rubber-burning of his own when faced with the unthinkable prospect of arriving late for a service in Christchurch Priory, and still with many miles between him in Wimborne and the priory. A rescue angel appeared in the form of an ambulance with flashing blue light, heading in the same direction. Chameleon-like, Sean turned on his own lights and followed in the ambulance's wake as all obstructions vaporised in their path. He arrived on time.

Health and Safety boffins should consider adding an organ in full cry to their Dangerous Species list. James Welch was at the helm when a conductor was taken by surprise:

> "When they put in a big new Casavant organ at Weidener Hall in Green Bay, Wisconsin, I was invited to play a recital for them, including the Widor V Symphony and the Saint-Saëns Symphony No. 3 with orchestra. The conductor was a man not well liked by the orchestra members. I had prepared the registrations for the organ part on my own.
>
> In the dress rehearsal we arrived at the point where the organ comes in with one of the most powerful C major chords ever written. I had been told to use the full power of the organ, so I did. The sound apparently startled the conductor so much that he lost his balance and fell backwards off the edge of the stage and into the seating below. It was a miracle that he was not injured, but it was all the orchestra could do to keep from applauding me. During the performance the next day, everyone held their breath when we reached that same chord. No repeat performance that time."

The Granada Cinema Organist Robinson Cleaver often left it to the last minute before getting down and on to the console for his show. Frank Fowler remembers that the lift gate would slam shut, the console would start coming up with Robbie starting his signature tune with one hand while scrambling on to the seat. At the Granada, in Tooting, Robbie had a platform with steps built by the lift. When he finished, he sent the console down, moving to the platform so that to the audience, he was left magically standing on thin air. He then took the applause and walked off down the platform steps.

> "He did not realise that on Thursday mornings the orchestra pit was cleaned and that the cleaners had shifted his platform and not put it back. Rushing in as usual for his performance all went well until he stepped off onto his platform. That night he beat the console down and he landed with a crash in the orchestra pit. Fortunately he did not hurt himself. The audience loved it, as did the manager, who wanted to keep this exit in until the end of the week. Robbie adopted a Queen Victoria attitude: he was not amused."

Just as the noise of the instrument can be used to good effect, the pipes can double as weapons. In a tragic incident in south London in 1999, policeman Tom Tracey had just been singing a psalm during Mass at St Andrew's Church in Thornton Heath, when a naked man burst in and attacked members of the congregation using a sword. Eleven people were taken to hospital, several critically injured, but it would have been even worse had Tom not downed his psalter, whipped a pipe from the organ and with the help of the congregation and a large crucifix, over-powered the man.

Adrian Taylor was honing his musical skills at Lyndhurst when it looked as if he might get more than just his technique sharpened by an unwelcome caller wielding a seriously large knife.

> "A chap came up and started chatting to me while I played. But the conversation made no sense whatsoever,

and I cannot remember the details, but if you imagine that I said 'good afternoon' and he replied with 'Shepherds pie', you get the idea. I quickly spotted he was a lump of mashed potato short of his shepherds pie, and tried to get away in a convenient interval while he wandered off to stare intently, rocking backwards and forwards, at a chunk of brickwork. Unfortunately, I did not manage to get my shoes back on before he had come to stand at the end of the choir stalls, blocking me; the organ console is at the end of the stalls, so the only way out is to either climb over or to walk down the whole length.

He talked to me about his time in the penguin colony or whatever, and I made polite noises, trying to manoeuvre past to escape. At which point I noticed he was holding a very large carving knife (one of those awful 'The World's Sharpest Knife' things that look like they were invented by a particularly psycho ex-Marine, designed for removing all vital organs with a single flick of the wrist) casually patting it against his leg.

Fortunately, after 45 minutes discussing the Martian cricket team, the poor guy's nasal haemorrhoids and the fact that he used to be a film star until the penguins started taking all his work, he wandered off. I then had to walk past the chunk of brick he'd been staring at — only to find a smelly yellow puddle to clear up."

A large blue flash shot out and up the pipes from the console, lighting the cathedral and the astonished faces of the hundreds of women gathered below.

Accidentals will happen

"A still-smouldering Philip quickly collared the dean and warned him they would have to use the draylon-covered piano."

A certain well-known (but shy enough to want to remain anonymous) organist had to play for an annual judges' service (while he was a cathedral assistant). The night before the service he had taken home his organ copy of the Howells *Collegium Regale*. He overslept and left the house in the Close in a hurry. He also left, unwittingly, his music. He went straight up to the organ loft and began to play the pre-service voluntaries.

> "The judges arrived in their finery looking ridiculous (I am not a fan of all that nonsense) and I remember mocking them from the loft. I got my come-uppance when it was time for the Te Deum. My colleague gave me two preparatory minim beats and the performance started. I was being very professional, and had my eyes glued to the mirror as well-trained, professional organists should do. I was sadly not professional enough to have remembered my copy, and gazed in horror at an empty music desk, and had to play the rest of the accompaniment from memory: not something I would readily do again, as it tested my powers of concentration and recall to a very high level indeed."

It took some prodding but after a few hours on my interviewing rack with the additional threat of disembowelment, Philip Smith confessed being accomplice to a case of carelessness bordering on vandalism. A certain Welsh cathedral organ, like many of its ilk, had been built, rebuilt, refiddled with, added to, dismembered, and was coming to the next session of tweaking. Plans were already underway. It was in this cathedral that the Mothers' Union of the diocese was celebrating its centenary, and two services were needed to accommodate the hordes of ladies, who sang lustily. Even the full organ (complete with Tuba) which was used for most of the service was barely heard. The afternoon service went without a hitch.

A choral scholar sat alongside Philip for the evening repeat service. During the sermon the organ was switched off. Towards the end of the sermon, the young man, getting fidgety, poked a pencil in the Hill, Norman and Beard starter keyhole of the blower. Result: the lead snapped off, stopping the starter key from being reinserted. Appalled, they looked at each other and the gummed-up hole, realising the sermon was about to give way to the next hymn. The scholar, in the optimistic way of youth, assured Philip that he could fix it and promptly removed the plate around the blower switch. The pencil lead was prised out but unfortunately so too were the live wires at the back of the blower hole. A large blue flash shot out and up the pipes from the console, lighting the cathedral and the astonished faces of the hundreds of women gathered below. The organ was dead and the pair in the loft a little singed, but alive.

A still-smouldering Philip quickly collared the dean and warned him they would have to use the draylon-covered piano on the other side of the crossing as the sole music-making contraption left to them. Even the honky-tonk rattle of this was unlikely to be audible above 1,000 warbling Welsh matrons, but they had to try. Seeing his career in smithereens, Philip stationed his choral scholar at the top end of the keyboard with instructions to thump out the melody as best he could. The lad was nothing if not obliging; he thumped with all the vigour he could muster. It was a pity that overcome by a fit of hysterics, he hammered out the melody not in octaves, but in fistfuls of hideous 7ths.

Immediately after walking on stage and taking his bow for a massed male voice choir event, Martin Setchell noticed the organ console TV monitor (his only means of reading the conductor's beat) was dead. He immediately climbed the stairs back out of the auditorium, called in the technician who unlocked the case-door with his keys, and entered the organ chamber to find the fault.

> "All was well, so I re-entered, took the keys from the case, automatically locked it again, and switched the organ back on. Just before the first item, I heard a frantic hammering from the tech now inadvertently imprisoned inside the case. I unlocked the door and he sprang out, with the presence of mind to take a huge bow to the audience. Guess who got the biggest round of applause that day. "

Before leaving Gloucester for studies at the Royal College of Music in London, Keith John was organist at the church of St Mary de Crypt, as was his father for many years before him. The organ was a solidly-built Victorian three manual with heavy tracker action, but it made a reasonably decent sound.

> "I thought I could improve it by pepping it up a bit, and duly located the pipes of the Harmonic Flute 4ft on the Great which, by moving them along a few holes on the soundboard, created a Twelfth $2\frac{2}{3}$. It worked and I thought it was wonderful; the pipes were not a perfect fit but I now had an 'exotic' stop.
>
> Inspired by this success, I wondered if I could improve the Pedal Organ a bit: there was a boring Violin 8ft which could possibly make a Quint $5\frac{1}{3}$. The pipes were rather larger this time but somehow I managed to reallocate them to new holes. Admittedly the result was not as impressive as the improvement to the Great but it was more interesting than what was there before. All was

> well for a time until one Sunday morning in the middle of a hymn, there was a loud crashing noise: some of my 'Quint' pipes had deposited themselves on to the floor and on subsequent inspection looked a little worse for wear. The rector was angry but did try to understand my explanation before calling in the tuner and banning me from interfering with the 'innards of the thing. Just play it!'."

After Ross Trant had been playing the organ at his church for some time, he convinced the minister and congregational leaders that the frequently malfunctioning, too-small console should be replaced. A second-hand three-manual Austin, everything on it working, was installed in its place. The stop keys were renamed and many of the original ones were removed as redundant, since the console had come from a much larger instrument. The Great and Swell occupied their traditional manuals, while the Choir was without stops in the new plan. Both Great and Swell could be coupled to it, at all three pitches, making it useful for fast registration changes. All the original couplers were maintained and operated within the console itself.

There was one unusual coupler, and it was called *Unisons On*. This appeared on each manual. Readers who play will be aware of the useful coupler, *Unisons Off*.

> "The night before the 'new' console was to be first demonstrated during a service, a friend and I went into the church and put the organ through its paces. My friend is a brilliant organist, so it was a delight to end our private musicale with his playing of the well-known Widor Toccata from the Fifth Symphony. As the last chord echoed in the lofty building, my friend pressed the general cancel. Two stop tabs remained in the On position, and he manually turned them off, closed the console, and I shut off the blower. We left."

Sunday morning was time for Ross to demonstrate the new acquisition. The blower responded instantly to the touch of the switch and the wind filled the reservoirs. The organ was alive. Or so he thought.

> "Usually the prelude to a service is quiet and chosen to set the mood for worship. Today, however, my plan was something more exciting. To show off the new console and make use of the third manual and all its couplers, I chose the chorale prelude on *Praise My Soul the King of Heaven*, a rousing work by Eugene Hill. The work was to begin with a mighty chord on the choir manual, Great and Swell both full and coupled at 16ft, 8ft, and 4ft pitches. Dead silence."

Appalled, Ross tried full Great with Swell coupled; this would be almost the same as planned, but without the 16ft Great coupler. Not a peep. The congregation, watching intently, became restless. He tried the Swell — at least with the reeds it would still be impressive. Still nothing, apart from a faint rumble from the Pedal Bourdon. The wind was on and it had been fine the night before. Ross was foxed.

> "Finally in desperation I went to the lowly upright piano, and did my best. After the service and profuse apologies to all who approached me, I returned to the console, and tried again. This time, the light dawned! *Swell Unisons On, Great Unisons On, Choir Unisons On*. All three were in the off position. None of these couplers was affected by the combination action or general cancel, and with good reason. When the tabs were moved, the organ sounded forth in all its glory, to a church empty of all but a red-faced organist."

But as we have all had to learn, it is not how you fall — it is how you pick yourself up. The difference between a truly class act and the bumbling amateur is the ability to keep going, despite derailments. In some cases, organists have made capital from it, as did Piet Kee when performing at St Peter's, Eaton Square, London. John Sayer was present when Piet had a glitch in the opening flourish of the (big) Bruhns E minor (little more than a split D#/E in the right hand or similar), from which he naturally recovered. But John reports that Piet had the last laugh:

> "When he got to the final item on his programme he did an improvisation in which he took as his theme the same mangled phrase from the beginning of the recital; a delightfully witty and self-deprecating touch much appreciated by the audience."

Whenever an organist marries it is written into the marriage service that his wife (or her husband) promises to honour, obey and turn pages without pay. Page turners (and here I speak as one who is so experienced that a solo page turning tour has been mooted) are a cross between the measles and a safety net. Organists love us, hate us, but need us. Try to dispense with us, and we will laugh the loudest when your scaled down, taped up, over-sized scores catch the draught from the open door and float away just as you come to that fiendish pedal passage.

Robert Bates spent a couple of years studying in Paris, during which time he became friends with Jesse Eschbach, another Francophile. Robert's friend Kimberly Marshall relays this incident:

> "Robert had a concert for which Jesse served as the page turner/registrant, and Robert forgot to warn him that his Bach scores were coming apart. He played the first page of the Bach G major BWV 541, and when Jesse turned, the page came off in his hands, flew out sideways and slid underneath the pedals. Jesse frantically tried to retrieve it with a pencil without interrupting the pedal runs that Robert was executing from memory. When Jesse finally managed to get the page up on the rack, Robert was already onto the third page, so all that effort was in vain."

Massimo Nosetti describes a recital that a friend of his, Richard Townend, gave at St Margaret Lothbury, London.

> "At the last minute, the usual page turner was unable to make it to a lunchtime recital. Hoping to get some help from somebody in the audience, Richard climbed down from the loft a few minutes before the recital to ask the people seated in the pews if somebody would be kind enough to help him by page turning. A middle-aged man volunteered.
>
> The two went up to the loft and, after a few practical details about how and when to turn the pages, Richard began his concert. Almost at the end of the second page, Richard nodded to the assistant who lifted the score from the music rack, put it carefully on his knees, turned the page ever so gently and slowly (in order to not rip it) and, finally, put the score back on the rack. The same happened thing happened for all other pages, to the horror of the astonished organist."

To be fair to assistants, page turning can be harder than playing the beast, especially when you are short. Certain organ consoles and benches (such as at Rochdale Town Hall in Lancashire) preclude anyone under two metres tall reaching the pages at all. James Lancelot chanced upon a novel way around the height problem as he was playing the anthem *Ascribe unto the Lord*.

> "We were nearing the end of the B minor men's quartet *They that make them*, ideally a soft interlude in an otherwise rather grand work. The small chorister who was turning my pages, unable to reach the music properly, elected to stand up to turn the page, planting himself firmly on pedal top F, the pedal section all nicely prepared *ff* for *As for our God, he is in heaven*. I did what anyone would have done: got hold of the boy's arm and pulled upwards until the noise stopped. Nowadays that would get one into severe trouble."

Occasionally, the format of printed music is a hidden problem. I turned pages for Gillian Weir in Christchurch Cathedral when she performed the premier of a work that had just won a national organ composition competition. The composer had the bright idea of assembling his many hand-written manuscript pages in concertina style. If opened out it would have measured several metres in length. I know that NOW. However, on that evening, unaware of the coil-sprung nature of the pages, I innocently turned the first page . . . and the remainder gracefully unfolded on Gillian's sequined feet.

Hand-Pumping Blowers

"I knew it was not my fault! It is all owing to your having played Gibbons, while I blowed Tallis"

In the centuries before electricity was invented, the wind supply to organs was delivered through bellows that were hand-pumped by organ blowers. Spare a thought for these denizens of the organ case who had to suffer the slips and fumbles of organists learning and practising, as well as attend to the needs of services and concerts. Even long after reservoirs were operated by electricity it took many decades for organs to be converted, so there are people living who have experienced, and survived, hand-pumped organs. Gerald Gifford is especially wise to their ways[10]:

> "Stories about human organ blowers are of course legion, and the following has been retold countless times, though it is perhaps useful to have an actual documentary reference for it. To judge by the date of the manuscript from which it is taken — c.1830 — it refers to an early nineteenth-century organist of Salisbury Cathedral, and probably to Arthur Thomas Corfe, who occupied this position from 1804 until 1863. The anonymous manuscript in question[11] is entitled *Organographia. Or a description of upwards of three Hundred*

10 Organists' Review 2004/2 Vol xc No 354, 130-131

11 RCM MS 1161 Royal College of Music, London.

of the most remarkable Church, Chapel and other Organs; in all parts of the world. With other curious information appertaining to these wonderful instruments. Perhaps, in view of the material that follows, the final sentence ought to have added *'and some of its players'*:

> 'A laughable circumstance of the importance of a former organ blower to this Cathedral, happened a few years ago, which we relate for the amusement of our Musical readers.
>
> The Te Deum and Jubilate, at morning service being set to music by different composers, and in different styles, it happens that they are of unequal lengths, which induced a former organ blower to amuse himself with counting the number of times he used to put down the bellows handles in each; from which practice he at length could tell exactly how many pumps he made for each Service. Hearing the boy, who usually comes to put up the Service[12], one morning mention Tallis's (one of the shortest), which was however changed by the organist for one that happened to be longer; he left off when he had completed the usual number of pumps; in consequence of which, a verse or two before the Te Deum concluded, the organ suddenly stopped for want of breath. On this, the Organist ran out to abuse the blower for his carelessness, when the blower, without seeming to think himself at all to blame, simply asked if Tallis's Service was not put up. "Tallis's!" says the Organist, "it was Gibbons's I played — but what the deuce is that to the purpose?" "Why there now," replied the other, "I knew it was not my fault! It is all owing to your having played Gibbons's, while I blowed Tallis's.'

In his autobiography, *Liebe zur Orgel* (*Beloved Organ* or *Love for the Organ*), Dutch-born organist-composer Gerard Bunk told of the difficulties in his youth when he wanted to practise the

12 The service music, presumably, on the organ console

organ. Bunk was appointed organist/director at the famous Walcker organ in the church of St Reinoldi in Dortmund, Germany in 1925, until his death in 1958. Gerard was allowed to practise in Scots Church in Rotterdam on a small historic Bevington organ. There he had to find a wind pumper for each of his practice sessions, which was not always easy. Sometimes no one was available, or Gerard did not have enough money to pay for him.

> "Therefore, you would have to help yourself. I would draw just one stop, like an Aeoline 8ft or Salicional 8ft, stops that don't need much wind. As a pedal stop, I would add a coupler only. Then, with all my might, I would pump the bellows to full capacity and in a split second, I would run as fast as possible to the console to play off the wind. However, this was not very long, and I had to start again to pump."

Later on, Gerard practised in a different church where the wind pumpers were men recruited from a nearby senior citizens home.

> "One old man did not charge much for his services. However, he seemed so weak on his skinny little legs, that I did not dare to draw more than an Aeoline-Salicional stop, otherwise he would stop pumping immediately. If I had drawn, in a youthful flush of excitement, a Mixture or Trumpet 8ft, he would knock at the wall which meant: 'Stop it immediately, or I will stop!' I would do a bashful diminuendo down to pianissimo. At the end of the practice session, when he received his meagre pay, he always complained that 'today the young man had used up a lot of wind.'
>
> In later years, I had a wind pumper for a recital who obviously knew something about music and looked at my music, maybe also to find out about how long he had still to pump. I remember that in the final piece, the Bach Toccata in D minor, during the last measures with all

> stops drawn, he disappeared, reckoning that the rest of the wind should be sufficient for the last notes. I nearly panicked, watching the indicator of the wind supply going down rapidly, so that I could not make a usual ritardando and I made the final chord very short since it had already gone down to a C-sharp minor chord."

The Rev. Augustus Toplady (1740-1778) recorded this event in the history of music at Worcester Cathedral:

> "At Worcester there was an idiot, who was employed at the cathedral there in blowing the organ. A remarkable fine anthem being performed one day, the organ blower, when all was over, said 'I think we have performed mighty well today.' 'We performed?' answered the organist, 'I think it was I performed; or I am much mistaken'. Shortly after, another celebrated piece of music was to be played. In the middle of the anthem the organ stops all at once. The organist[13], cries out in a passion, 'Why do you not blow?' The fellow, on that, pops out his head from behind the organ and says 'Shall it be we?'."

Even though organ pumpers had been replaced by electric motors, inventiveness was still needed. Robert Bowles tells of a peculiar blowing accessory in the organ loft of Bedford School Chapel: a steam locomotive. It was only an 00 scale Kitmaster plastic model, so it did not steam, but it had a job to do. It ran on a length of track across the top of the music desk. Its position indicated the amount in the reservoir.

> "The organ had originally been hand-blown but an electric blower had been installed. The string and weight, which had told the person doing the pumping how full the reservoir was, had been diverted across the top of the music desk with some extra pulleys, and the engine was attached to the string. The pneumatic action was full of

13 probably Isaac Elias who held the post 1747 — 93

leaks and some ranks had been added, so it was not very difficult to empty the reservoirs. It was a very useful tool.

The master who installed this arrangement had moved on by my time, leaving behind a single black locomotive. I understood there had previously been a whole set painted in various colours, which he changed around so that the locomotive was always the correct liturgical colour for the season. He was, apparently, quite keen on trains."

Critically speaking

"The choir were in another postal district and I had a mirror the size of a 10p piece."

If organists happen to be practising in a church where the organ console is accessible to the congregation or visitors, they soon encounter interested passers-by, who fit into one of two categories. Either they are experts on all matters musical and especially on the pieces being rehearsed, and would very much like to offer their advice to the player. Or they are bemused by an organ and bursting with curiosity to learn — without delay — how it works.

At Altenberg Cathedral in Germany I photographed a procession of both categories filing past Martin Setchell as he tried to concentrate on the registration for an imminent concert, and the resultant 30-odd shots resembled the characters from a Breugel painting. I have pictures of the disgruntled family who angrily left after their request for *Ave Maria* was politely rejected because of the lack of rehearsal time. I also took many photos of those who stood watching as close as they could get, breathing down Martin's neck as he tried to concentrate. But the one shot that was potentially the best of the lot I missed simply because it was so unexpected. An enthusiast, having stood beside the organ bench for some time, suddenly leaned over to thumb through the pages of the score from which Martin was playing. Ouch. . .

On one occasion while practising a transcription of the Tchaikovsky *Nutcracker* suite at his local church, Keith John was shouted at by an angry woman "How dare you play this circus music in church!". By contrast, when Keith recorded it in Reykjavik, the church administrator danced around the church whenever she came in and heard him playing it. As Gerard Brooks was practising *Dieu Parmi Nous* from Messiaen's *Nativité*, an outraged gentleman who was visiting went to speak to him: "Of course, I hope you are never going to play that sort of music in church. . . "

For some, the volume is hard to adjust to. A farmer at First Lutheran Church, Williston, North Dakota complained to Faythe Freese after she had played Messiaen's *Apparition de l'Eglise Eternelle* that Occupational Safety and Health Administration would not let him run his gravel crusher that loud.

Audiences are not always as discerning as we would wish. John Wells was asked to play at a French hospice in the Bordeaux region. He was a little nervous about playing for folk with mental impairment but was reassured that they would be a friendly and appreciative audience. And they were. Much gratified by their enthusiastic applause, John expressed his satisfaction to the warden after the concert.

> "Yes, they love to come," the Warden agreed, "but it is the clapping they really love, n'est-ce pas? They really love clapping. You could get up there and blow your nose and they would still clap."

Some organ repertoire is equally adored and hated. David Rothe experienced both reactions when playing Messiaen's *Apparition de l'Eglise Eternelle.* At a concert at California State University, Chico, a young man went up to him and told him that he had a life-changing religious experience while listening. He indeed became a devout follower (and later, leader) of a well-meaning, non-traditional semi-religious group, and became a faithful member of the university chorus.

"I also played the piece as a prelude for the First United Methodist Congregation in Oroville, CA. After the service a little old lady came up to me during the coffee hour and asked: 'What was that piece that you played for the prelude this morning?' I told her, and she replied, 'Please do not ever play that piece here again.' I did not, because I truly believe that she would have kicked me in the shin if I had dared to play it again."

Organists are often asked their opinion of an instrument, and it pays to be diplomatic. Not like a former assistant organist at an English cathedral who went with the cathedral choir to sing Evensong elsewhere in the city. The church had an organ that was a patchwork effort, and the so-called builder of the instrument was the then current organist (and organ fanatic), who had collected parts of redundant instruments and done a DIY job. After struggling to get anything out of this awful collection of pipes and electrical circuitry, the hapless visiting organist was not at all impressed.

"The Choir were in another postal district and I had a mirror the size of a 10p piece by which to see my colleague's beat (all the repertoire was accompanied and difficult: Leighton and some fast Handel). There was also a disaster with one of the hymns — *Hail Thee, Festival Day* — with choir, organ and congregation performing different verses at the same time to different parts of the tune. The result was similar to something the great Karl Stockhausen had penned.

After the service finished and I had played the voluntary, people were waxing lyrical about the triumphant performance of the choir and how wonderful the organ sounded. The organist and some members of the congregation asked me what I thought of the organ. I had already told my boss what I thought of it, and he was standing by me when the deputation asked this contentious question. I remained silent and my boss very tact-

> fully said that he thought that it was very nice. 'How could it be improved?' persisted the deputation. My less than tactful response was 'I think that some petrol and a box of matches ought to do the trick'. I never went back."

Working for the Church is full of surprises. The vicar of an Anglican church in New Zealand unilaterally chose to use an untrained music leader, and an amateur organist regularly for the main morning worship service. This naturally upset the appointed professional organist as well as breaching his contract.

> At a meeting intended to solve this contentious issue, the vicar told the organist: "The trouble with you is that you're a perfectionist — your music is too good. How do you think it makes the man in the pew feel?"
>
> The organist was aghast. "I'm sorry; I thought the whole idea was to offer only my best efforts to the glory of God. I'm trying to aid worship as well as I can."
>
> He paused, and hoping to lighten the tense atmosphere, added as something of a joke: "Perhaps I should make some mistakes — play a few wrong notes, use the wrong tune, that sort of thing. Would that make people feel better?" To the musician's astonishment, the vicar's face brightened for the first time in the meeting.
>
> "Well, yes, actually, that would help. Yes, a good idea — play some wrong notes."

It was at that sorry point the organist realised that after 50 years, he and the Church would have to part company.

And they did.

Teachers, pupils and simply children

"Flare nostrils!" "Heave bosom!" "Suffer!" "Snarl like a dog with a bone!"

I explain that it was because I could no longer afford the lessons; he claims it was because he needed a page turner and registrant on tap; whatever the reason, my organ teacher and I married; a happily symbiotic relationship that we have found to be reasonably common in the music world. It also means that any nuclear domestic debate has to be postponed until after concerts. With a regular schedule of engagements I think we should work our way to our 90th anniversary. (Memo to organists: be nice; be very, very nice to your page turners. They can do a lot of damage.)

It is worth remembering that even the legendary players have all been pupils at one time. Even Peter Hurford. Peter's wife Pat used to help Peter balance the registration before concerts by listening from where an audience would be seated. At St Michael's church in Framlingham, Suffolk, when Peter was preparing for a concert as part of the Aldeburgh Festival, Pat had to shout up to Peter in the loft that the pedal was too loud, the flutes were too soft, or similar registration-balancing comments. An elderly woman approached her with an air of considerable respect. "Are you his teacher?" she whispered. I suppose in a way she was.

David Rumsey was invited to be a jury member at the Rueil-Malmaison Conservatoire in Paris as the final-year organ students competed for the "premier prix". Xavier Darasse and Jean Langlais were also on the jury.

> "After one student had played a Bach Prelude and Fugue with little or no registration change, Langlais, evidently disturbed by this, got up, mid-exam, and called out with great French 'precision' in his tone: 'I demand to know: who taught you to play like that?'
>
> "The baffled student was reduced to silence (and possibly tears) when, after a second or two, a rescuing voice came out of the church saying 'I did'. It was Marie-Claire Alain. Langlais sat down, the student recovered and went on. Shop-talk over the lunch which ensued was amazingly wide-ranging, but for some reason registration of Bach was not once mentioned."

Like it or not, teachers often have the perfect solution for a range of musical conundrums. Olivier Messiaen was complaining that organists played his work, *Le Banquet Céleste*, too fast. He asked his teacher Marcel Dupré, "Maestro, organists play *Le Banquet Céleste* too fast. How can I stop them from doing that?" Dupré answered, "All you have to do is to rewrite it in longer note values." So that is why two editions of this work exist, the second edition containing longer note values than the first. The semiquavers (sixteenth notes) are transformed into quavers (eighth notes), the quavers into crotchets (quarter notes), the crotchets into minims (half notes), and the minims into semibreves (whole notes).

Teachers can also have a profound influence in our lives. As a schoolboy of 14, Frank Fowler was one of three budding organists wheeled in to play a piece to Reginald Foort, the pre-war BBC staff theatre organist, when he was to give a recital at the local chapel.

> "After Mr Foort had finished rehearsing we were trooped in. He was sitting in shirtsleeves at the console. He immediately gave us his famous smile, and said, 'Come on over, boys' We approached clutching our music and he said 'There is not much point in you playing

> to me, I have heard a lot of playing in my time. How about me playing for you and you asking me questions. You will learn far more listening to me than me listening to you'."
>
> We did, and thus spent an hour of fascinating instruction. He taught me a lesson that I have remembered all my life. If there is someone more expert than you who is willing to offer information and advice, shut up, listen, and learn."

Later in his career as an organ builder, Frank met Eric Thiman frequently, and was present when Eric invited members of the visiting organists' association to play to him.

> "After a string of 'ear bashers', a youngster got on the organ and managed to play more loudly that anyone else before him. When Dr Thiman had had enough, he got up, walked slowly to the console, put his arm round the youngster's shoulders. The boy stopped suddenly in mid *ffff* with surprise, to hear Dr Thiman's still, small voice, nevertheless carrying throughout the whole church, saying 'You know my boy, you will find some soft stops on the organ if you look hard enough for them'."

In Canada Healey Willan was a hero for many aspiring organists, accomplished ones as well. Ross Trant was one such student:

> "He was always welcoming when young people visited him in the gallery, and took time to explain the console and features of the instrument to which he always referred as The Old Girl. On the rare occasions that his playing was not up to his own liking, he would comment, 'The old girl was a bit out of sorts this morning.' He was always very pleased to hear people say to him after the Mass 'The old girl sounded very well today, Doctor'."

Proving that it is not what you say, it is how you say it, the best teachers have got their message across in novel and colourful ways. Raphaël Tambyeff tells of Edouard Souberbielle, a pupil of Louis Vierne and Eugène Gigout, who was Professor of Organ at the Ecole César Franck (a private music school offering a high level curriculum) in Paris. He taught many organists who are now famous, such as Michel Chapuis and André Isoir.

> "One day during a master class, a lady wearing a hat was playing the organ with a very agitated posture. When she finished playing, Edouard said 'Mademoiselle, if your hat had little bells on it, we would have heard an authentic carillon.' That was his way of reproaching the pupil's agitated posture. Perhaps it was something about the female organist that got to Edouard. During a master class a woman played the fugue from Bach's Toccata, Adagio and Fugue in C Major in a very detached manner. Edouard told her 'Madame, that piece is lace; do not put holes in it'."

James Welch treasures the scores marked by his Stanford University teacher Herbert Nanney:

> "I may have been pretty good at playing the notes, but my first lessons with him showed me how much more there was to music. I have saved the comments he wrote in my musical scores to get me to play more effectively: 'Flare nostrils!' 'Heave bosom! Suffer! Snarl like a dog with a bone'!"

As well as coping with clergy, congregations, choirs and playing the music, an organist is a magnet for children: their own, and everyone else's. Free-range children pose perhaps the biggest danger to organists trying to concentrate on the matter in hand. Timothy Tikker encountered such a child early on in his service-playing career.

> "I was playing a postlude at my home church in San Francisco, when a little boy, perhaps three to four years

old, came running up and greeted me with an enthusiastic "hello!". I murmured a greeting back at him. Then he clambered onto the bench with me, and started to whack the upper part of the main manual with the flat of his hand — this on nearly full organ. I managed to stop playing long enough to grab the boy, and half-place, half-hurl him onto the floor, then go back to the postlude. He landed in a heap, and ran away, presumably to his otherwise quite inattentive parents. Some well-meaning bystander then remarked on the humor of the incident to me as I continued playing, and attempted to concentrate on same.

After the service, I told several people what had happened; it turned out that none of them had noticed anything out of the ordinary whatsoever."

In the spring of 1991, Pamela Decker's late first husband, Bill Albright (who taught for many years at the University of Michigan), substituted for Pamela for two Sundays at her new church position at St James' Episcopal Church in Dexter, MI. The church had a lovely, historically noteworthy building — small and cozy, but ornate and beautiful. There was an historic Henry Erben one-manual (full pedal) pipe organ that was quite visible in the chancel area.

"I am just under 5'2" and petite. Bill was about seven or eight inches taller and he was a much more substantial, powerful-looking person when seated at the console of a tiny historic instrument bearing only one manual. Anyone who played was prominently visible to everyone in the church."

Bill told me about what had happened during the children's sermon at St James while I was gone. He was seated at the Erben, politely following the sermon, which was conducted as a question-and-answer method. Father Harry asked the children which item was new in the chancel area of the church. One child singled out something that had been part of the chancel for some time, so the question was repeated. Again, a child mentioned something that was a regular feature. Then, the rector said, 'Okay, what is new in the chancel area that is REALLY BIG?' A little boy raised his hand and bounced eagerly, saying, 'I know, I know. . .', so Harry called on him. The little boy pointed straight at Bill, saying, 'That man playing the organ'!"

Nigel Ogden, presenter of the BBC Radio 2 programme *The Organist Entertains*, counts himself privileged, in the late 1960s and early 1970s, to have gained early theatre organ experience by providing pre-show, interval and exit music on the four-manual, 14-rank Wurlitzer in the Gaumont Theatre in Manchester. A couple of hundred yards away, on the other side of Oxford Street, was another equally fine art deco picture palace, the city's Odeon, with an even larger Wurlitzer of four manuals and 20 ranks of pipes.

"A delightful chap by the name of Ronnie Wood had been house organist at the Odeon since the early 1950s and, as his organ spots tended to be scheduled a few minutes later than mine at the Gaumont, on Saturday evenings I would finish my first interlude then nip across the road and stand at the back of the Odeon stalls to listen to Ronnie, after which we would meet for a drink and a chat before it was time for us both to play again.

I vividly remember listening to Ronnie playing a particularly fine medley of 1930s foxtrots during the ice-cream interval when I became aware of a diminutive, cheeky-faced urchin about seven or eight years old walking down the aisle towards the organ console which was, of course, raised up on its lift platform bathed in spotlight.

"With his wooden spoon, the objectionable child extracted a lump of best vanilla and raspberry from the tub of ice-cream he was carrying and flicked it with admirable dexterity onto Ronnie's back. This would have been unfortunate enough if Ronnie had been wearing, as was normally his custom, a white tuxedo. However, on this occasion — wouldn't you know it? — he had chosen to appear in a navy blue suit so the effect of the foodstuff's arrival on his jacket was dramatic.

Initially, the boy's actions produced no noticeable reaction, at least as far as the organist, concentrating on the job in hand, was concerned. It was only when the boy's mother rushed down the aisle, produced a handkerchief and started rubbing vigorously at Ronnie's recently embellished tailoring that events took even more of a downward turn. I have never seen such a sequence of emotions as those that passed over Ronnie's face during those next few seconds as he tried to work out what was going on. I have also never heard that delightful old song, *Love Is The Sweetest Thing*, rendered with such feeling, and such interesting harmonies."

The Ignorant – blissful and otherwise

"Look! He's playing music by hand!"

Organists spend their adult life (and no doubt a good deal of pubescent life) wearily responding to nudge-nudge, wink-wink jokes by titillated lay people who become hysterical when the word organ is mentioned. "So, (chortle, snicker, splutter) that means (gurgle, snort, guffaw) you have the biggest (choke, giggle, hoot) organ in town!" Yawn. Very droll. Yes, you are the 156,092nd person to mention that.

The depths of ignorance plunge further — much further. To non-organ buffs, a large pipe organ and how it works is as fathomable as 10-dimensional topography or Towser's Logic. Worse, they do not even know that they do not know how complex it is. A city organist was once asked by a town hall staff member if he could take the organ outside the auditorium to be tuned because they needed the hall for a piano tuning.

Educating the masses who hitherto had considered organs only as parts of a body has been a quite a mission for the Christchurch musical community. Peter Harty, a doctor by day, was one of the thousands of supporters who nursed the Christchurch Rieger through conception, gestation, and birth. He thought that his own family at least knew what sort of baby they were dealing with. But he was to get a little surprise from a well-educated relative when she attended a Polytechnic graduation ceremony in the town hall, soon after the Rieger installation.

> "She had not seen the organ before and when she entered the auditorium she gasped in surprise at the sight of all the façade pipes lit in blue and red. She then swooned at its amazing sound, and turning to my wife, said, 'How awesome! Does it take long to pack it all up afterwards'?"

Russell Kent was poised to start a solo piece on the same town hall organ at a Christchurch School of Music concert when a woman rushed up with a microphone on a stand, thrust it past Russell, placing it near the manuals. Asked what she was doing, she said "We are recording the concert." Confused, he asked why she was shoving the microphone up to the keyboard. She said "Well, that's where the sound comes out, isn't it?" Russell told her to take her contraption much further away, and suggested that the foyer outside the auditorium would be the perfect spot.

While at the University of California, Santa Barbara, James Welch was asked to demonstrate the Flentrop organ for a big music appreciation class.

> "I played some Bach for them, and when I started, a young woman behind me said quite audibly, 'Look! He's playing music by hand!' I guess it had never occurred to her that music could come out of anything but loud-speakers, and was produced somehow mysteriously."

One evening Michael Whitehall dropped into a country pub at Swinscoe, a village on the Derbyshire-Staffordshire border. At the bar he got into conversation with a farmer who, finding that he was an organist, told him that he had recently bought an organ for his daughter to play. Suspecting that it would be an instrument of the 'entertainment' variety Michael asked about the compass of the keyboards. The farmer could not supply details but he did at least know the name, and assured Michael "It is one of the best — it's a Wertiliser".

Clergy — working closely with organs and organists as many do — should know better. But Massimo Nosetti discovered that is not always the case. The main fan of the air conditioning system in a church in Italy failed on a hot summer Sunday while Massimo was playing. As soon as the priest realised that the temperature was rising he sent the verger to the organ loft asking Massimo to play as much as possible with the lower pedals. Massimo was puzzled; why would that help? The priest replied that the air coming out from the big 16-foot pipes would help a little to keep the room cool.

Organs confuse even organists. A rustic local organist from a nearby village came closer to inspect the rather garish casework of the new organ while Gerard Brooks was practising at St Andrew's University Chapel. The visitor was not impressed. Wandering round towards the back, he found the swell shutters, which are at ground level. "What is all this in here?" he asked, "spares?"

American composer Daniel Gawthrop relates a story he heard from the late Vincent E. Slater when he was about to take up his first church position. The church had experienced the unexpected death of their organist-choirmaster and had hired Vincent after a hasty phone interview. During the several weeks between their former organist's death and Vincent's arrival, playing duties had fallen upon an elderly lady whose only organ qualification was many faithful years as a Sunday School pianist.

> "I arrived at the church and was introduced to this sweet soul, who kindly took me to the console of their modest two-manual instrument and proceeded to show me its features and explain its intricacies. As part of the 'tour' she insisted on drawing each stop in turn, alone, and playing a few notes on it. I listened patiently through the entire stoplist. Last of all, she drew a three-rank mixture. After playing a few notes on it she turned to me and said, 'I hardly ever use this Chinese stop'."

Family members dragooned into playing for a wedding are usually out of their depth. A British organist had a call from his priest to say that the family 'organist' for an impending marriage had come to practise, and wanted a word. The priest put the woman on the line: "Oh, hi. I can't find the rhythm section."

Non-musical, non-organic, normal people can be forgiven for not knowing their chamades from their chalumeaux, and comments from such visitors on hearing the sound of the organ in great cathedrals can brighten many a dull tour session. During the day, when Chester Cathedral was crowded with visitors, Roger Fisher often rehearsed silently (like Marie-Madeleine Duruflé, who strongly advocated practising 'without the sound'). One summer afternoon the cathedral was crowded, and the following conversation took place:

> Intense American lady: "Why is he playing away up there and there's no sound coming out?"
>
> Elderly Verger: "You see, Madam, he's practising a recital for the deaf and dumb."
>
> Intense American lady: "How kind. . . "

Even the most well-intentioned, earnest types can trip up. Roy Massey was invited to play a recital at a church in Birmingham near where he used to live as a boy. As was customary in this church, a chairman was appointed for the evening to introduce him, and to propose a vote of thanks at the end.

> "The lovely man who was on duty that night was obviously not an extempore speaker, as everything he said was written down in advance and solemnly read out. Unfortunately, the organ was not a very good one, having been built by a cheap local firm, and something went terribly wrong in the middle of the concert. I tried my best to sort it out but, eventually, had to tell the audience that I had 'broken their organ' and could not finish the programme. They seemed slightly dazed, so the chairman stood up, took his script out of his pocket and solemnly read: 'I am sure you would like me to express

my gratitude to Dr Massey for what he has done for us this evening.' At this, there was an enormous outburst of laughter from the audience and the poor chap, looking bewildered, realised the irony of what he had just read."

A long line of people waited to greet Marilyn Mason, doyen of organ teaching for more than 60 years, after a recital in the Riverside Church, New York City. Marilyn was thrilled to see many new and old friends, and she tried to spend a short time with each visitor. A woman came up, planted herself squarely in front of her and addressed her:

"Oh, Miss Mason, I just envy you!"

"Yes?"

She repeated, louder, "I just ENVY YOU!" (Marilyn wanted to ask if she envied all those hours of evening and early morning times when she had to practise relentlessly.)

"YOU ARE SO LUCKY!" Marilyn had had enough and bellowed back: "Yes, the more I PRACTISE the LUCKIER I get!"

When Fred Swann was organist at that same Riverside Church in New York City, a woman approached him one Sunday after church, asking if he felt "worn out." He said he did not, and she remarked: "Well, I am surprised! You usually let that organ just roar, and this morning during communion it was so soft and beautiful. Did not it take all the strength you had to hold back all the usual loud sound?"

Women organists have probably all met the same surprised reaction as I have when listeners – if they have been unaware who was playing – have discovered the musician to be female.

"My goodness! You're a woman!" (yes...) "Wow! Amazing how much sound you got out of that thing just now..." (Yeh, right...). If you are diminutive, the astonishment is proportionately greater. Members of a congregation would often tell me that they could not understand how such "enormous sounds could be made by such a little person". I could never could resist such comments.

"Just you wait until I'm all growed up," I'd usually reply, tugging at imaginary plaits and sucking a thumb. . .

Organically challenged vicars trying to be helpful are a menace. Paul Carr met one such in Hereford when he was presenting a short series of words-and-music concerts with the writer Alick Rowe.

> "Alick was the main attraction and told wonderful stories; I was there to put in sound effects, dramatic chords at creepy moments, and to play one or two pieces that fitted in with the moods he had so excellently created. It had been successful elsewhere, and the next was to be in Hereford. I had used the two-manual Willis on the West end gallery for practice while I was organ scholar at the cathedral around the corner a few years before. Because it was straight-forward, and knowing the organ well, I did not go to rehearse until about an hour before the concert.
>
> "On arrival I found that not only had the organ gone, but so had the whole gallery, and all of the pews, as part of the major re-ordering of the church. The Willis, since re-built at the side of the church, was spread out in pieces down the side aisle. We were greeted by the vicar who, seeing my shocked reaction, said, 'We will be using the Lady Chapel organ this evening, and I have wheeled it out for you'.
>
> The Lady Chapel organ was a one-manual, no pedals, two rank (Dulciana and Stopped Flute) pipe organ about the size of an upright piano with the pipes literally sticking out of the top. The two ranks were both available, via stop tabs, at 16ft (TC) 8ft, 4ft, 2 2/3, 2ft, but the ranks were not extended, so it was a pretty rough sound.

The icing on the cake was that the vicar, looking rather pleased with himself, had straightened the stoppers on the tops of the pipes. He had thought they were all 'looking untidy', which is just what it did to the tuning. I do not remember much after that — I think I have blanked it from my mind. We did the concert and I must have coped somehow."

Most organists have to tolerate a fair amount of word-play teasing about their choice of career, but truly delightful moments come from innocuous comments by those who should, but do not, know better. Colin Mitchell and others witnessed the visit of a straight-laced female organist of a Methodist church, who had gone to play a substantial four-manual Harrison in Halifax. She tootled around for half-an-hour and thoroughly enjoyed herself. It was then time for a small group to retire to the 'vestry' for a couple of pints, but she decided not to join them. As they stood chatting, she thanked them for the chance to play. Colin continues:

> "Now this lady not only looked like, but had a voice exactly like that of the late Hilda Baker. Taking her leave, she said, 'Eee, do you know, my organ's only a little one, but it gives me so much pleasure. Ooh, but yer know, it's grand to get your hands on a big one like yours' The tears of laughter were still rolling when we finally arrived at the 'vestry'."

Not all innocents are harmless. The downright dangerous types are so ignorant that they do not know enough to keep their paws off the workings of an instrument. Graham Dukes' nemesis was a chap called, shall we say, Arthur.

> "I was playing at a church that had no money for anything, let alone repairs to the organ. It was an ancient tracker that I suspect had been defective from the start, and had got no better after 60 years. Having enjoyed a medical training, I got into the habit of remedying its most acute defects with surgical plaster (on the bellows),

> forceps (to remove dead bats and suchlike) and self-adhesive bandage (to tie up anything loose).
>
> Arthur was an odd-job man who would, free of charge, do little things like change burnt-out lamps in the nave, tidy up, and toll the bell when no-one else was around to do it. But I was increasingly suspicious that he was getting ideas about tackling the organ, just as he tackled washing machines and bicycles.
>
> The day came when, turning up early for practice, I found myself playing some wrong notes while depressing the right keys. Sure enough, Arthur (who had a key to the church) had found evidence of my having stopped a leakage on the windchest by stuffing paper around a couple of pipes, and felt he could make a better job of it. Having taken out a couple of pipes to get better access, he had replaced them in the wrong holes, interchanging D and E flat. Pipes are pipes, aren't they, so what does it matter where they go? I bought a padlock for the door to the organ loft next day."

The best-laid plans of mice and architects go oft astray. Gareth Perkins tells the sad history of a church that was built in the 1960s to serve a new housing estate. Soon afterwards, the authorities realised the architect had forgotten to make allowance for an organ chamber. This, unfortunately, was discovered only after the church had been built. Therefore they demolished part of the brand new church — as one does — so an organ could be installed.

> "Then a few years back, the church building was closed for a couple of months for it to be reorganised. The church was divided into two by a solid wall. One half of it was to be kept for worship, the other half to serve as a new community hall. It was only after the wall was built, dividing the building in two, that some bright spark realised the organ had been overlooked. The organ had been left in the community hall part, and there was

> no room for it in the section set aside for worship. I understand that they are still having to sing unaccompanied."

Concert organisers can be just as appallingly unenlightened. Raúl Prieto Ramírez in Barcelona got a phone call from, let's say, a Mr Z asking him about his Thursday concert programme in Valencia. This surprised Raúl, because it was Tuesday, and he knew nothing about any concert, let alone that it was in Valencia. But it had been announced six months ago, protested Mr Z. (The concert had been booked by *Jeunesses Musicales* in Valencia without consultation with Raúl — no phone call, no email, no carrier pigeon — nothing.)

Since publicity had already been distributed, the concert would have to go ahead. Raúl asked Mr Z for details about the organ. "Which organ do you mean?" asked a startled Mr Z. "We have no organ, that's your problem; you have to bring the organ yourself." In Valencia an organist always carries his own organ for concerts, he claimed. Raúl argued that professional pipe organists did not supply their own organ, but it did not impress Mr Z. He grumpily lectured Raúl: "You are much too young to ask so much".

A few blandishments later, and after being offered various alternative instruments, Raúl agreed to play, but only on condition it was a pipe organ. Mr Z phoned him later to explain that he had found one in a church in front of the hall. Raúl asked him for the organ specifications so he could plan the programme.

> "He told me this: 56 manuals and 30 pedals (such a huge organ!) Fortunately I had that afternoon free so I took a train from Barcelona and I arrived just one hour before the concert. When I saw the organ, its pedal compass was only 27 notes for a small unit system electric organ, no bigger than a simple wardrobe. I had to transpose many pedal passages meant for a 30-note pedal compass, but anyway I played the concert, with not a bad result."

Some months later a friend told Raúl that Mr Z had spread rumours that Raúl was an arrogant young man, who wanted too much. "What can I do if he does not understand that an organist needs at least an organ to play? Perhaps he is such a great conductor that he can conduct a Brahms symphony without an orchestra?"

Organists have been known to foul things up through their own blissful innocence. In early 1999 there was a pre-election rally of green groups in the Sydney Town Hall. As far as the City Organist Robert Ampt was concerned, he was merely leaving his briefcase in the town hall while waiting for the rally to finish before he started his organ practise. However, to the environmental activists who noticed him leaving the briefcase, Rob was obviously a terrorist, and his case contained a bomb.

As a result, the police were alerted, and 1,500 people evacuated from the town hall. The music case in fact contained sheet music, organ shoes, contact lens holder, a banana, and — most vitally of all — no bomb. Rob, far from being a subversive, protested his obliviousness to the potential threat by labelling himself as a "home renovator and gardener. I don't like violence at all; I never watch the violent bits on TV."[14]

14 Ampt. ibid. p.141

Maybe apocryphal, maybe not

"He then had a uniquely attentive audience when, after the third piece, he took out his teeth and placed them on the console."

A weird instrument understandably attracts weird characters. Having been around for more centuries than many instruments, the organ has accumulated devotees who have cultivated and embellished legends that are now already set in stone. Here follow a few that might not have made it into the organist's bible. They may, or may not, be true. Most tales from the organ loft that have appeared in journals and books, internet chat group forums such as the Mander discussion group in the UK or PIPORG-L chat in the USA, have at least a grounding in truth. Some yarns may be merely whimsical fancies, yet make enjoyable reading when taken with a twitch of the tremulant.

Almost every organist of any repute appears to be credited with this (or a very similar) witty response to a classic idiocy. The story goes that during a service, the presiding minister (as they do) announced "The organ will now play". In silence, the organist remained on the bench, in silence. The minister repeated: "The organ will now play". Organist: "Then let it!"

Sometimes specific characters gather about them a cloud of anecdotes that get passed from organist to organist. Todd Wilson relates second-hand a story about the redoubtable Clair Coci who was playing a recital in a church where the chancel had two identical doorways, one on each side. One door led to the rest of the building, the other to a very tiny sacristy closet with no other exit. Not knowing the building well, at the interval Clair went through the closet door and remained in this tiny space for a full 15-minute intermission, at the end of which she came out smiling and unruffled, to the great amusement of those who knew the building.

Legend has it that George Thalben-Ball, of Temple Church, London fame, had only the thinnest veil behind which he hid his contempt for the organist of the City Temple Eric Thiman. George was invited to play for wedding at The City Temple (where there was a large Walker organ), but Eric, as the incumbent, insisted on accompanying the choir, and playing the wedding marches and hymns. George was therefore relegated to the role of assistant organist, playing only the voluntaries. So George hatched a plot. When the signal came that the bride had arrived, Eric hurriedly slipped on to the organ bench and blindly stabbed at the thumb-pistons as he looked towards the door. The bride entered, less than impressively, to an opening fanfare played on the 8ft Great Flute with Swell Celestes coupled. George had reversed all the thumb-pistons.

According to Philip Wells, Guillaume Ormond, when he was the cathedral organist at Truro, was out sailing somewhere in Cornwall. Ormond realised he would be too late for Evensong, so he sent a telegram to the cathedral saying he could not get back. The Truro postman did not know how or where to deliver it, so walked in through the west door, up the nave to the chancel, and delivered it to the cleric taking Evensong that day. Ormond was also very forgetful, adds Gareth Perkins. Ormond had once absent-mindedly taken all the copies of an anthem upstairs to the loft and discovered his mistake only during 'Lighten our Darkness'. It was too late to go downstairs and so the whole lot was jettisoned over the side to the choristers waiting below. It is said that, more than once, he would drive somewhere to go shopping, forget that he had driven there, and return home by train. On finding his car missing, he would phone the police to report the 'theft'.

Enough versions of the following story indicate that there may well be a foundation of truth to them. Sir William McKie, when organist of Westminster Abbey between 1941 and 1963, visited the Cathedral of St John the Divine in New York. He was not over-happy. First, they called him 'Sir Bill' and second they took great delight in pointing out that everything was larger (but not older) than Westminster Abbey. Eventually they arrived beneath the great circular West window, with its battery of reed pipes *en chamade*.

"Say, Sir Bill," they said, "That's our State Trumpet, bet you haven't got anything like that back at the Abbey". Sir William looked at them coldly and replied "When we want the State Trumpets, we send for them."

Another eminent character was Sidney Campbell, who is remembered now as much for his sayings and antics as his playing. David Harrison relates the story of Sidney visiting the Isle of Man, where his predecessor Marmaduke Conway had retired. Marmaduke and his wife took Sidney for an afternoon drive, and they chanced upon a wayside restaurant that looked suitable for afternoon tea. The proprietor, as he saw them approach, jumped up and immediately wound up an enormous horn gramophone and started a record. It was greeted by Marmaduke with "Oh, do turn that off; we none of us like music."

Colin Mitchell passes on the definitely fictional tale about the time that Sidney Campbell was assistant to Marmaduke Conway in 1949. Marmaduke left the choir under Sidney's direction for the anthem during Evensong, so that he could be in the organ loft in time to play the final voluntary. He began the voluntary, then a few minutes later an ear-splitting cacophony from the organ startled worshippers. Marmaduke, the story goes, had died, and lay slumped over the keyboard. Sidney Campbell climbed into the organ loft and pulled the dead organist off the organ, placing his body in the corner. Sidney continued playing the voluntary, during which time the ambulance men arrived in the organ loft and looked blankly at him. Allegedly Sidney, while still playing, nodded towards the corner and said, in his usual, dry voice, "The dead one is over there." [15]

Sidney Campbell certainly had a way with words. Peter Clark has heard that Sidney was once asked, when at Southwark Cathedral, "What is the cathedral for?" to which he replied "To keep the organ dry". David Wyld contributed another story of Sidney, organist of Ely Cathedral from 1949 to 1953, when an aged, somnambulant Canon once began intoning immediately after the Magnificat: "I believe in God. . ." Retort from Sidney in the loft: "So do I, but we will have the Nunc Dimittis first, shall we?"

Conrad Eden was similarly quick-witted. He once drove Alan Thurlow to a Royal School of Church Music event in Darlington on a Saturday. Finding nowhere to park, he pulled up in an office car park. A porter came running out and said to Conrad "Excuse me, this is a private car park!". To which Conrad replied, "That is fine, my good man. This is a private car."

In her graduation address upon receiving an Honorary Doctorate in 2002 from the University of Central England in Birmingham, Gillian Weir had a plausible tale of the dangers of modern technology:

> "No doubt this will be the first time many of you have actually seen an organist in person, since we are often hidden away in an organ loft hanging like a gargoyle from the rafters. Recently an attempt was made to rectify that situation in a cathedral in Europe, and a closed circuit television camera and screen were set up so that the audience could see the organist play.
>
> Unfortunately they did not think to tell the performer. It was a warm night, and after the first piece he removed his jacket. After the second piece — it was very warm — he took off his tie. He then had a uniquely attentive

15 Marmaduke Conway in fact died in the Isle of Man

audience when, after the third piece, he took out his teeth and placed them on the console."

Colin Mitchell tells of the organist who was invited to a fancy-dress party organised by parish members as a fund-raising exercise. Children went as ghouls and witches, Little Red Riding Hood, princesses, scary animals and, in one case, as a little red devil with pointed tail and horns. The adults, less successfully, went variously as Farmer Giles, monks, nuns, the Grim Reaper, and other well-hackneyed objects of curiosity.

"One of the adults arrived dressed convincingly as Count Dracula; having gone to great lengths to do justice to his role. He had plastic fangs, a black cape hired from a theatrical shop, smeared fake blood around his mouth, and even gone to the discomfort of obtaining clear-red contact lenses. The whole thing was realistic, and quite alarming; some children burst into tears as he bared his teeth at them and breathed huskily. It was not so much human blood on which he imbibed, more 'Bull's Blood', but it was red and alcoholic enough, which was all that mattered.

By the end of the evening, many people were a little worse for wear as they departed in taxis. Count Dracula was only a student at the time, and therefore queued for the last bus into town, rather drunk, swaying perilously and with the cape drawn tightly around his body against the cold. With blurred vision from the powerful effects of the Bull's Blood, Count Dracula almost missed his stop. Making an inebriated lunge, he launched himself towards the stairs of the open-platform, double-decker bus, tripping on his black cape and plunging headlong down them. Barely touching the rear platform of the old bus, Count Dracula bounced onto the pavement in a crumpled heap. Quite unconcerned, the bus conductor rang the bell and the bus set off, leaving Dracula lying dazed on the pavement.

A few moments later, the living dead was discovered by a policeman on the beat, but at the same time, a passing taxi came to a halt, and various princes, potentates and one Tom Thumb leapt out, having recognised Count Dracula lying there semi-concious. The policeman did not do much to assist the afflicted but as he grasped for his radio, he looked upwards, searching for the name of the street. Instead, he saw the brass plate on the door. It announced that the building outside which Count Dracula lay slumped and dazed was used as the offices and collection clinic of the local Blood Transfusion Service.

The policeman's face turned a slightly whiter shade of pale, but the fellow fancy dress party goers reassured him. 'It's all right,' said one, 'it's just our church organist. He has had a bit to drink.' Count Dracula, with almost full conscience regained, fixed his red eyes upon the constable, opened his mouth, bared his fangs and confirmed his identity with a husky, 'Aye'."

The dodgy side

"I promptly threw up into his music case"

Despite rumours to the contrary, organists do have failings, and organ lofts and pubs are often interchangeable venues. A shining example of an organ built to accommodate human frailty is the Rieger in Ratzeburg Cathedral. When the Rauschwerk stopknob is pulled, a drinks cabinet in the console pops out. (Rauschwerk is a pun, meaning both a reed stop or a stop sounding like a reed, and also meaning roaring drunk in German.) No wonder that Rieger Orgelbau playfully notated the stop in the organ specification as being 'for high fidelity'.

A similar contraption provides for thirsty players at St Paul's, Newcastle-under-Lyme. Originally a Hill, the instrument was rebuilt by George Sixsmith and Sons, and boasts a tempting Tibia Liquida. When drawn, it reveals a miniature cocktail cabinet with interior lighting. Lead crystal glasses and a selection of miniature tinctures complete the idyllic scene. This concession to the foibles of organists is rare because most disgraceful behaviour happens well before — and after — they lay hands on a stop knob.

Luckily for him, an organist who wishes to remain untraceable, fell from grace when he was well away from the console. Mr B was in Cambridge for the day with a friend, playing for a visiting organists' association in St John's College, having been a recent organ scholar there.

"We were met later in the Baron of Beef by George Guest who greeted my friend very warmly, and serious drinking started. I was about 20, but even I could not keep up with the arrival of pints. I had a nearly full one and another waiting when George bought another round, so I changed to shorts. A couple of rounds later and I had caught up on the pint-front, but now had about three double scotches sitting in front of me. The rest of the evening is a bit of a blur, but I remember the start of the journey home, sitting on the two-car diesel Sprinter train with the engine vibrating the entire carriage, the smell of diesel fumes, and feeling very unwell.

Apparently what happened next was that I turned to my friend, said his name, at which he stopped going through the music in his attaché case on his lap and looked at me. I promptly threw up into his music case. He has for years told me I owe him a copy of *Dieu Parmi Nous* that took the full brunt."

Frederick Geoghegan (a prominent British-trained figure in Canadian organ music) enjoyed a bit of a drink, reports Christopher Dawes, and he disappeared before a funeral he was to have played. As near as anyone has been able to reconstruct, he passed out at the console, probably on the pedals. No-one thought to look there, and the funeral went ahead without music. It is said that Frederick regained consciousness at the blessing, near the end of the service, and not fully realising the situation, but knowing something had to be done, made a quick decision. He pressed a general piston and launched into the Wedding March from Mendelssohn's *Midsummer Night's Dream*.

Accidents are not always self-inflicted. In 2006 Katherine Dienes-Williams had gastroenteritis during her practice session for a recital in St Paul's Cathedral, London. Katherine soon realised she was not going to make it down to the crypt bathroom in time, and she had to improvise with materials to hand. The organ loft rubbish bin will never be quite the same.

Behaviour in places of worship varies according to the culture. Visiting organs in the Netherlands, Colin Mitchell was often taken aback to find a church caretaker mopping floors with a cigarette in his mouth. In the more important venues, people would sit in church to read a book, enjoy a cup of coffee and smoke a cigarette or a pipe. He recalls seeing a notice on the organ of the Waalsekerk, Amsterdam (the Muller organ where Gustav Leonhardt was the organist), which read in both Dutch and English, "No smoking at the console please." (Even the sacrosanct organ of the Royal Albert Hall once had a well-used ashtray on the console; burn-marks in the wood attested to inattention by the smoker while playing a longer piece than usual.)

> "The biggest surprise was when the wife of my host, wandering around a small, but exquisite country church, took out a clay pipe and proceeded to puff on the most acrid of blends, sending plumes of blue smoke into the air. Considering how priceless the organs are, and also many of the paintings by old masters in so many churches, I could never quite reconcile the smoking with the effect it may be having on such treasures. I was not too bothered about the religious aspects, because I tend to agree with the view that the church is just a building like any other, and the spiritual temple is that of humanity."

Every vocation harbours dodgy characters and the organ world has its fair share of those who are one pipe short of a rank. An overseas organist touring New Zealand was puzzled by a simple chunk of wood nailed to the head of his bed. His curiosity overcame shyness and he pressed his hosts for the story behind its presence. A previous organist, they explained, had left an irremovable hair-grease stain on the wallpaper. They had solved the problem by simply hammering a plank of wood over the offending mark. Of greater concern to the hosts was a stash of gin bottles found another time underneath the same bed.

During his tenure as organist and choir master at St Laurence's Parish Church, Ludlow, Shropshire, Richard Francis organised a weekly series of recitals, sometimes given by distinguished celebrities, and sometimes by slightly less able players. Among the latter was a certain doctor (not of music) in the 1990s who claimed to be a specialist in 18th century organ music. He proceeded to play a complete recital without using his feet at any point.

> "Having guided us through Anon (Dutch), Girolamo Cavazzoni, and William Byrd, he paused for a long time. Thinking he had been taken ill, I rushed up to the organ to find the gentleman vigorously rubbing his right thigh to remove the agonising cramp that had set in. I heard him exclaim in desperation, 'Good God, I do not know why I inflict this misery and pain upon myself and such a forbearing audience' (about six people). He managed to finish off with pieces by Stanley and Handel, and disappeared to join his host, never to be seen again."

During the 1970s, one organist was notorious for playing recitals in Germany that he called Kreuzstab Konzerte (Cross Staff recitals), so named after Bach's Cantata No. 56, *Ich will den Kreuzstab gerne tragen* (*I will carry the cross gladly*). It was rumoured that he had been miraculously healed from a deadly disease. As a result he had decided to play for benefit organ recitals, and to donate the money to charitable institutions. Hans Hielscher says that Mr X only improvised, and never played organ literature in his recitals.

> "I remember that he did this well; he could improvise in true Bach style and in all pre-Bach styles. Moreover, he brought along several other instruments, such as a recorder, a flute, a trumpet, or more exotic ones like a Macedonian pan flute. In the middle of a programme he would ask the audience to name a favourite hymn tune or folksong. Then he would play ex-tempore one of his solo instruments, and accompany himself with one hand,

or feet only. This certainly made a great impression on the audiences. At the end of the recital, they gave generous donations for 'a bicycle in Uganda, Africa' or 'medication for a missionary station in Afghanistan', or whatever Mr X had asked for at the beginning of his 'benefit' recital."

Mr X's frugal method of approaching his fellow organists to arrange concert dates doubtless irritated his local Post Office. Often he sent his letters in a used envelope with an invalidated stamp, crossing out the previous addressee and replacing it with the new address. He even used old official postal service cards or letters, such as those for phone bills, scribbling his note somewhere on them, then dropping them in a mailbox, minus a stamp. Or, to ensure he got a quick reply, he prepared a sheet of paper, with weekdays written one below the other on one part, months on the second part and all hours on the third section. Then he asked the recipient to mark or to tear off the respective date and hour, and return it to him.

But the anxieties he caused the Post Office were nothing to the trail of palpitating concert organisers in his wake because of his fondness for arriving at the very last minute.

> "When I first met him," says Hans, "I was concerned when he had not arrived an hour beforehand. I hurried to print a new programme, expecting that I would have to play a substitute concert myself. Then, at the last minute, he appeared. I accompanied him to the console, he sat down, and I was just about to explain to him the functions of the console, when he put his foot on the pedal board and began to play."

On another occasion, Mr X was supposed to play on one of the East Frisian islands in the North Sea where the infrequent ferry boat service depends on the tides. He arrived at the ferry boat terminal on the mainland only to find that the last boat had left two hours before. Aware that he had to play on the island in two hours, he chose to walk there, over the mudflats. Fortunately, it was ebb-tide, but nevertheless a risky attempt. When he came to the narrow channels of water, he held his Macedonian pan flute above his head, and swam.

> "Believe it or not, he made the church in time and played his recital after changing his wet clothes in the vicarage. It took several years before mistrustful vicars and suspicious listeners found out that he never passed their donations to the promised recipients. As far as I know, he disappeared from the organ scene in the late 1970s and was sentenced to jail. He has not been seen since."

Merely musing

"The mourners had all come upstairs, leaving 'Mama' outside in the ice and snow."

The organ has so many voices other than the triumphal, loud, even pompous sound that people naturally associate with it. Given the right registration, it can be playful or soporific. It can dance, laugh, imitate other instruments, and suit so many moods and occasions. It is the oldest instrument around, and it runs the gamut of human emotion in a way which is too deep for words. The organ is a fickle potentate that can crush towering egos in one flash of mechanical instability, yet smugly laud its architectural beauty for tourist cameras. Organs really should carry health warnings.

Why do organists decide to devote their lives to this temperamental titan? Christopher Herrick is one who has devoted more hours than most. Here is how he began:

> "It was the sheer majesty and brilliance of the St Paul's Cathedral organ, in the hands of the organist Sir John Dykes Bower, that made me decide that 'this is what I really want to do!' I was 12 years old and a chorister at St Paul's. Sir John had invited me to turn pages for him one evening when he was recording a programme for the BBC. On that occasion he used the full panoply of big trumpet stops in what was for him an un-

characteristically flamboyant manner. For me it was a 'road to Damascus' conversion. In all the ensuing years, I have never for one moment regretted the hours and hours of organ playing that have resulted from that decision to try and tame and make sense of that wonderful musical/mechanical beast."

Once in a while those of us who are passionate about the instrument and its music are fortunate enough to witness such a life-changing experience as described by Christopher. I recall watching a young lad about five years old who sat spell-bound with his father through an evening solo organ concert in the Christchurch Town Hall. He did not squeak or jiggle in the manner of small boys, but sat, open-mouthed, drinking in the sounds. At the end I commented to the father on this and thanked him for bringing the boy to the concert as he obviously had enjoyed it so much. The father laughed. "I didn't bring him; he's already been to the mid-day concert for schools today and he insisted that I had to come with him tonight."

Bagpipes and the organ have a lot in common: passions run high whether you love or loathe the instrument in question. For some people they both have the power to move the listener — as far away as possible. It is conceivable that detractors may not have heard the right catalyst music and have yet to be converted. My own conversion experience was hearing Bach's Trio Sonata in C minor played on a bubbly tracker action. Then, for the first time, I heard the composer giggling, a little tipsy, delighting in the joy of writing such witty music.

Organists themselves are occasionally surprised at the effect their playing can have on listeners. Kimberly Marshall was teaching a student at Memorial Church, Stanford, and had forgotten to lock the downstairs door to the organ gallery. A dishevelled middle-aged woman came up the stairs silently and nearly scared teacher and pupil to death when she approached them at the console. She explained what she wanted:

> "My mother died a few days ago. They are holding the funeral today, but I cannot be there. Can you please play a hymn (she mentioned one unfamiliar to Kimberly) so that I can be with them in spirit?"

Kimberly found the tune in the hymnal, while the woman went back downstairs to listen.

> "I played it through several times on different meditative registrations. Then we resumed the lesson. As organists, we hold a vital power to move the spirits of our listeners, and there have been few times when I felt that power so acutely."

David Rumsey was asked to deputise at the last minute at a necropolis in Basel (see page 14), and the family had requested, at the last minute, the Bach Fantasia and Fugue in G minor.

> "Next day I did some more practice and had the fantasia well under control. The fugue was still a bit shaky, but I figured that, by the time I had played the first page, they would all have disappeared and I could relax. The service concluded and I launched forth on the fugue. Sure enough, to my relief, the mourners quickly disappeared.
>
> I completed the fugue and in the relaxed atmosphere of playing it to an empty chapel it went well. Arriving at the great tierce de picardie at the end I was about to collect my belongings and leave, when a thunderous applause broke out from directly behind me in the gallery. The mourners had all come upstairs, leaving 'Mama' outside in the ice and snow. The son said "Thanks — that is our family's favourite fugue", tipped me an additional amount that more than doubled my expectations, and they all (someone whistling the theme) left, collected Mama, and disappeared into the graveyard."

Cherry Rhodes learned about the universal power of music when she gave a concert tour in Czechoslovakia while a student in Paris in 1968.

> "I have never seen such appreciative people. They were so hungry for music; but they were also hungry to see an American. It was a symbol of freedom for them — just to be with an American gave them so much joy. After the recitals, people would form two lines outside the churches creating a path so I could walk among them. It was unbelievable. People would bring flowers, little gifts and tokens of the city, paintings and so on. I will never forget a cute, darling couple, maybe in their late teens, who gave me a little sailor made out of sponges. None of these people even knew of me, but I was a musician and an American. After the recitals, I would go into a restaurant and everybody would recognise and acknowledge me. You do not experience that in the United States unless you are some kind of rock-star."

Nina De Sole takes pleasure from playing the organ in a church that has stained glass windows.

> "At sunset, to feel and see the colours and the rays of sun with the music makes it a special experience. Another thing I enjoy is playing when the church is in complete darkness, and there's only you and the organ, lit by the lamps on top of the music rack and pedal board. One recommendation though: bring a flashlight for your way back."

A number of years ago Gerald Gifford was invited to record an album of trumpet and organ music with the distinguished British trumpet player Crispian Steele-Perkins.

> "We were very fortunate to get Hexham Abbey, Northumberland, with its magnificent Phelps organ for the recording, even though the location (in the centre of a busy market town) meant that we had to record

> overnight. We were all excited at the prospect of being the first to record the Vivaldi Concerto for Two Trumpets with a single soloist, and accordingly Crispian began by playing the first trumpet part; I played an orchestral reduction on the organ. He then dubbed the second trumpet part, and I — as a particularly novel experience — played continuo with myself. By the time that this happy state was successfully accomplished, it was about 3.30 am. Crispian wanted to add a few refinements to one or other of his solo parts, so I decided to find a quiet side chapel, and take a nap stretched out on one of the pews.
>
> It is a curiously unnerving experience to awake suddenly from such a posture, bathed by the gently luminescent glow of ancient stained glass, while hearing the distant sound of a single trumpeter."

In spite of the fact that Roman Krasnovsky plays the organ in famous cathedrals all over the world, in Israel his day job is that of a garbage collector. One time he performed in the famous Cologne Cathedral, Germany.

> "No need to explain what it means for an organist to play in Cologne Cathedral. Among various pieces on my programme I also played my own *Jewish Symphony* for organ. It was a great success and I was told that there were more that 2,000 people in the audience. After the concert, we went to a restaurant to celebrate. The people that joined us complimented me on my performance.
>
> During the meal I raised a glass of wine for a toast, and said: "For me, of course, playing the organ in Cologne Cathedral is a unique and a special event, but for the Cologne Cathedral it is also a special day today, because, it never happened before that a Jewish symphony was played by a garbage collector from Israel."

Organs Behaving badly

Ciphers, crescendo pedals or just plain weird

". . . a splendidly be-gowned verger appeared carrying a big red fire extinguisher, with the words 'you might need this, sir."

The bigger the occasion, the more likely the darlings are to spit their pipes. For instance, at the Madrid Concert Hall, Keith John had an important concert that was to be broadcast live. He sweated through the preparation and had already spent 12 hours on the programme that included his transcription of Tchaikovsky's *Nutcracker Suite*. The combination system was an 'interesting' one which he thought he had the measure of, but suddenly the whole lot vanished and there was nothing he could do to bring it all back.

"Helpful administrative people produced a book on the wretched system but, as it was all in Spanish, it was as good as useless to me. I tried phoning the builder without success, and so then contacted the organist who arranged the concerts, who had to make a long journey

> in to central Madrid to help. To everyone's relief she arrived and managed to find all the lost combination settings."

Tchaikovsky and his Nutcracker had not finished with Keith and returned to plague him, this time in full cry at Fairfield Hall in Croydon, England.

> "Suddenly some curious electrical gremlin struck the combination system and for a few agonisingly long seconds there was silence. I jabbed at the full organ button to get something to sound which it eventually did and I finished the concert without daring to touch another piston of any kind."

An organ acting true to form will misbehave less than 24 hours before an important event, so it is often impossible to diagnose and repair the problem quickly.

Soon after David Willcocks succeeded Walter Alcock as organist of Salisbury Cathedral in 1947, he was to play the organ during a live BBC radio broadcast. He had noticed the day before that one of the organ notes stuck whenever he played it. His wife Rachel was meant to be turning pages for him, and together they devised a plan to avoid disaster during the broadcast.

> "She sat in the swell-box right by the faulty pallet, and whenever I played it, she would quickly push it back down. The plan worked brilliantly. I cannot now recall which note it was, but I remember that I played it at least a dozen times, and, despite the dusty, cramped conditions in the swell-box, Rachel successfully stopped it every time."

While recording the Prelude to Wagner's *Die Meistersinger* on the Mormon Tabernacle organ in 1998, Richard Elliott discovered to his dismay that the pitch of the Swell division was sagging slightly on the final C major chords, resulting in a 'grand celeste.'

"The organ has an excellent wind supply, but I had piled on additional stops and notes for the final chord, not realising that what had worked well in live performances was not quite as effective in a recording. After scratching our heads over a possible solution, the head organ technician, Robert Poll, volunteered to position himself next to the regulator for the lower end of the Swell division in order to operate the curtain valve manually each time the chord was played. A trial run proved to be successful, and we rolled tape with Robert dutifully tugging on the curtain valve cord in rhythm with the final blasts of the organ.

When putting together the credits for the CD booklet, it occurred to me that Robert's contribution went beyond the normal call of duty and needed to be recognised in some way. Those who bought the '*How Sweet the Sound*' CD (now out of print) were either mystified or amused by the note under the Prelude to Die Meistersinger: 'Final chord features Robert Poll, Der Meistermagazinbalghochheber'.[16]"

At the Sydney Opera House through the 1980s and beyond, the organ would suddenly get it into its head to do a quick and spontaneous crescendo.

David Rumsey recalls he would be playing on a couple of soft stops when, unexpectedly, the organ would crescendo to maximum. Within one to two seconds the softly beguiling celestes would transform into a cacophonous screeching of mixtures, reeds, and chamades. On a good day the player would see the three-digit read-out suddenly start rolling upwards and get a foot to the crescendo pedal, reverse it, hopefully with minimal musical damage. As a result, performances tended to be on a knife edge.

16 This very loosely translates as "Master magazine bellows high-lifter"

"Once, during the Strauss *Alpine Symphony*, at a little three-bar organ solo towards the end marked *mf*, then *p* then *pp* (as the horns entered accompanied by the organ) I had my eyes on the conductor and missed the unprovoked escalation of the read-out. A lot of stunned people listened as the organ, instead of a gentle foundational 8ft *mf* entered with a devastating *fff* with reeds and upper work ablaze (at least it covered the organist's expletives). It then moved by the next bar to an unexpected *ff* — *diminuendo* and arrived at the required *pp* just as the conductor brought the horns in, conducting them with his right hand. With his left, however, he made a magnificent mime of wiping his brow, lips pursed in a silent 'phew'."

It would be fair to say that David Rumsey has been jinxed by organs in the Sydney Opera House. Sometime in the mid 1970s, while waiting for the Grand Organ to become playable, he had to use an electronic organ for a performance of *The Planets* Suite by Holst. In addition to what was already in David's part, the conductor asked him to play an open 5th on C and G with all he could muster on the pedals at 32ft and 16ft pitch for the end of *Mars*.

"The rehearsals went well, but at the first performance there was suddenly an unbelievable, massive rumble at this point. We were all nonplussed, but kept our cool and the performance continued. I was not playing in the next movement so I looked around and soon found the problem: the organ's transposition read-out was down a major third. So instead of a neat open fifth we had a massive A flat secondary seventh chord at 32ft pitch. I snapped the control back to its rightful place and the rest of the concert went without problem."

The cause? "The organ part never brought my hands anywhere near the transposing facility and the beginning had been at the correct pitch. I have a hunch it was electrical interference of some kind, but to this day it has not been explained."

Since Pierre Cochereau's time as titulaire at Notre Dame de Paris, it has been the custom for guest organists to prepare registrations for the Sunday recital on Friday night, then to tape the programme the following night (Saturday). This routine worked well until in the early 1990s, when the Notre Dame organ underwent a rebuild and the console was equipped with state-of-the-art devices. Many new and unusual electronic gadgets made it sometimes very unreliable.

It was in that period that Hans Hielscher was engaged to play a recital. He worked on his registrations for some hours on Friday night and set the pistons.

> "When I returned on Saturday night to record the programme, all settings were gone, deleted. So I had to start again to re-set all combinations as far as I could remember of what I had done the previous night. That took quite a long time, and at the end, when we began to tape the programme, parts of the pedal notes did not work. Although the stops were drawn, there were at least 10 'dead' notes. It took us several takes with different pedal registrations to get the music on tape."

With mixed feelings Hans approached the organ the next day, Sunday, half an hour before the concert. Recitalists are not allowed to play even a single note before the recital at 5.45 pm because of the many activities in the cathedral.

> "But when I pushed the pistons silently, just to double-check what I had set — again the same disaster as the night before: everything was gone! Since I had not made any handwritten notes of these registrations (it would have taken too long for a huge organ like that), I tried to think of alternatives, and not to panic."

One of the titulaires, Olivier Latry, arrived in time to hear the disastrous news. He was highly sympathetic, exasperated and angry at the ongoing problems with the organ. He offered to cancel the concert and explain the matter to the audience. Hans was determined to continue.

> "I remembered that on the previous nights the stops were working when drawn by hand, except for occasional pedal notes. So I played, treating the huge instrument like a mechanical stop action organ, and using the general crescendo pedal often. I guess that very few in the audience noticed that anything was wrong."

Soon after this weekend, the recital series and the use of the Grand Orgue in the services were interrupted for more than a year as the console underwent several checks and repair work. When Hans played again in Notre Dame, the grand old dame behaved herself.

It's easy to spot organists. Just say the word 'cipher' and watch the reaction. Organists will turn ghostly hue and flinch as if being hit by a wet 64ft Untersatz. Everyone — but everyone — who plays has experienced a note that refuses to stop sounding. Christopher Herrick:

> "The last service I played accompanying the choir at Westminster Abbey turned into something of a nightmare. The anthem, Parry's *I was glad*, seemed a fairly standard way to make an exit. But the organ had a will of its own, perhaps getting its own back on all those endless evening hours of practice. Halfway through the anthem an unstoppable cipher developed on the high B flat on all the Swell stops. As you can imagine, I was NOT glad!"

As a college student, Roger Fisher was playing for a performance of Mendelssohn's *Elijah* by the Woodford and Wanstead Choral Society. The performance got a much-needed kick up the bass line in the chorus *Baal, we cry to thee*. At the words "hear and answer" Baal answered back in the form of a cipher on the Tuba.

Roger had to go into the organ and remove the pipe before the performance could continue.

Organs reserve some of their best tantrums for performances of Messiah; consider it to be the organ equivalent of Shakespeare's 'Scottish play'. I once rehearsed Messiah stoically for two weeks, and only hours before the performance everything that could make a noise, made it. After some hasty recalculations, the concert went ahead with all stops cancelled, bar one 8ft flute rank that alone was behaving itself. And mere hours after the feeble bleatings of sheep going widely astray had faded, the organ was back to normal.

James Lancelot was playing organ continuo at Winchester Cathedral and the performance had reached the moment in the *Amen* chorus where the choir rests and the violins re-enter on their own.

> "Unfortunately the previous pedal note chose to cipher on the Contra Bombard 32ft (yes, I am afraid it was that sort of performance). Fortunately the Bombard rank was (uniquely) on a ventil, operated by an old bakelite switch somewhere down by the pedal board; after an agonising number of bars the note ran out of wind, with a noise like a motorbike roaring off into the distance. Great was the surprise downstairs when the organ re-entered with the chorus, Bombard-less but otherwise in full majesty. Everyone assumed I had had to switch off the wind and go home."

Hans Hielscher had recitals on the island of Sardinia in the Mediterranean, and one was in the small city of Lanusei. The abbey church had a modest-size two-manual organ on the west gallery, with the electric console placed in the chancel, some 55 metres away. Hans immediately discovered an unusual problem: all pedals sounded a half-tone higher than the manual keys, which sounded at the correct pitch.

"Just imagine: you play a C major chord with your hands which sounds, of course, in C major. Then you play with your foot a C on the pedal board, and it sounds C sharp. I do not have any problems with transposing, as we all have to do this. But have you ever tried to sing a tune in F and accompany yourself in F sharp? This exactly was the problem in Lanusei."

A malfunction in the electric system was probably the culprit, but it could not be repaired at short notice, especially on a Sunday afternoon, in a small city in the middle of nowhere. One of the monks suggested cancelling the recital and sending the audience home. Although appalled at the difficulties the schizophrenic tunings presented, Hans wanted the concert to go ahead.

"There are always solutions to such problems. In this case, the solution was simple: instead of the pedal stops, I used the pedal couplers for the pedal part only. At least they worked correctly. So I played all the scheduled pieces of my programme, using the pedal couplers. Occasionally, for cadenzas and final notes, I used even some of the real pedal stops, concentrating on playing the 'wrong' note a semitone lower.

I still wonder why they invited me there for a recital on an organ that was not working properly. Maybe the organist was a pianist who did not use the pedals at all, and never realised that his pedal board was pitched too high? I will never know."

Computers, gadgets and even electricity can not be blamed in many cases; good old mechanical parts can throw a cause red faces as Philip Bailey found when he was singing in Fauré's Requiem in west London.

"During the Libera Me I discovered that the main reservoir went back up with a squeak, so it came out "Li-i-[squeak]-be-ra [squeak] me Do-o-[squeak]-mi-ne [squeak]" — all through. The choir was in hysterics. It has to be the worst performance ever of that movement, and all because of the boink-boink-pause chord writing."

Roy Massey's first association with the organ loft at Hereford Cathedral was inauspicious. He had been appointed Organist and Master of the Choristers in April, 1974 and visited the cathedral to have a look round. Evensong was due and Roy took his place at the side of the console to watch.

"Soon after the assistant organist started to play, smoke began to issue from beneath the bottom row of keys. He continued playing, with the remark that 'it doesn't usually do this' and valiantly carried on with the service. The choir was singing Wood in D and Psalm 104 (which contains the very apt line 'if he do but touch the hills they shall smoke.') Half way through, a splendidly be-gowned verger appeared with a big red fire extinguisher with the words 'you might need this, sir', though neither of us had any idea how to work the thing.

By the end of the service there was a pall of black smoke in the vaulting. The dean and a canon or two appeared in the loft immediately afterwards wondering what had happened. I said to the dean, 'I think your organ needs rebuilding' and he reluctantly had to agree although he had no idea where funds for such an enterprise might come from. Fortunately, Bulmers, the local cider-making firm came to our rescue two years later and paid for the Father Willis to be splendidly rebuilt by Harrison and Harrison of Durham."

The organ at Nelson Cathedral was wheezing asthmatically and barely emitting any sound when Tim Bell played it, although the action seemed fine. The cause was an electrician working on the cathedral wiring, who had inadvertently swapped the phases on the three-phase motor, subsequently running in reverse.

(Reverse wiring has happened surprisingly often, and one instance has been recorded for posterity, quite literally. A CD recording artist was told — post-production, post-release, post-everything — that exactly the same kind of reverse wiring had resulted in a weak sucking, not blowing, organ in his recording.)

Occasionally, the organ is entirely innocent of charges of malevolence. Pity the poor builder who unfairly gets the blame for a hiccuping behemoth. The affectionately nicknamed Voice of Jupiter monster in the Royal Albert Hall had been silent for two years while being rebuilt by Mander Organs, so the musical world gurgled with impatience to hear it anew. Splendid gala solo concerts celebrating the reopening in June 2004 went smoothly. The first chance for the organ to impress the promenading masses with its 147 stops and 9997 speaking pipes a few weeks later was keenly anticipated.

So on the night of the BBC Proms, Jupiter sat there, looking gorgeous and basking in its £1.7 million makeover. The trouble was, that was all it did. Not a peep escaped its pipes, and organist Martin Neary had to play the organ part for Charles Ives' Fourth Symphony on a Yamaha P-250 instead.

Although a pall of embarrassment descended over the hall, the fault was nothing to do with the organ, the builders, or the player; an over-enthusiastic electrician had switched off something he should not have. So with the mere flick of a switch the beast and its blowers were ready for the Proms next day.

"Out it came, all two feet of it, just as the stop-knob said. . ."

Noises off and stops on

"All 61 notes on the tuba ciphered at the same time."

Few listeners to Mary Mozelle's frequently requested recording of Dan Gawthrop's music on Organlive.com would have been aware of the pressures under which she made it. Mary had saved for years to make a commercial solo CD and the opportunity finally came to use the Mander pipe organ in Princeton University Chapel, Princeton NJ. It took her months to make arrangements for the recording dates, set for June, 2006. She travelled to Princeton a month ahead to set up the registrations and arrange for the rental of the chapel. Mary organised the organ curator to tune beforehand and to stay around during the recording sessions in case there were problems. She made hotel reservations, and co-ordinated all the details with the recording engineer. She was ultra-organised, in every sense. It was going to be a wonderful experience, she knew it.

On 14 June, as she approached, Mary saw construction fences around the north side of the beautiful gothic chapel. Large trucks and heavy equipment were tearing up the concrete and stone sidewalks; jackhammers joyfully rat-a-tatted a welcome; trucks reversing to a building just behind the chapel beep-beep-beep-beeped in antiphonal ecstasy. They were so happy to see her.

> "I nearly had a heart attack. The normally quiet and idyllic Princeton University campus had been turned into a noisy, dirty construction zone, right next to the chapel. How on earth could I record the next two days with all of this? We all know that during a recording session we must strive to have the most absolutely quiet environment possible! At first I panicked, of course, but then I contacted the university organist to beg for some kind of help, especially since I would be paying $1000 a day for the use of the space for recording."

The story ends happily. The pavement workers (jackhammers and other heavy equipment) were scheduled to work somewhere else on campus for the next two days and they obliged willingly. Unfortunately, the trucks had been hired for that week and needed to complete the work on schedule. Nothing could change that.

> "So my engineer-producer and I planned to get most of our work done while the trucks were loading, then stop when they were backing up. As the recording sessions progressed, the trucks and their awful beep beep beep interfered with the recording a few times. We had to do multiple takes of some of the quiet endings to get one without the beep. In the end the recording turned out just fine. I have a few more grey hairs now than I had before the recording, however.
>
> The organ curator did not have to tune a single pipe during the entire recording session, but on the very first day of recording, he did have to fix the squeaky bench. Yes, believe it or not, that darned bench was so noisy that we had to stop several times and do another take because of the interference."

Getting the necessary silence for recording in a cathedral or church requires great planning, patience, and the odd public transport timetable. The Anglican Cathedral in Christchurch, New Zealand, is in the hub of the busy square which until recently was the congregating point for the city bus line. The building was therefore surrounded by at least six bus stops. Every 10 minutes an eager exhaust-belching bus would screech to a halt, slam doors open and shut, then vroom off into the distance. Recording a Widor programme for Radio New Zealand, Martin Setchell had to play with a city transport timetable on the music desk, so he could stop and start according to the scheduled bus arrivals and departures.

At Westminster Abbey, Christopher Herrick had similar worries. It was his first recording, *Organ Fireworks from Westminster Abbey*, that was to lead to more than 20 years collaboration with Hyperion Records.

> "I am proud, and looking back, slightly amazed to have recorded this disc during a single three-hour session. This was annoyingly interrupted halfway through by a bell practice in the adjacent tower of St Margaret's Church. Though the recording was digital, Hyperion issued it at first as a black disc with the CD following a bit later. CDs were then still a novelty. It is curious and revealing that listening on first-class equipment, it is possible to hear a tiny bit of bell-ringing sound in one of the echoes on the CD but not on the black disc."

Although minuscule by comparison, the natty little key finder given to Robert (Bob) Elms proved almost as irritating. The petulant gizmo chirped if, having mislaid it, the owner whistled. New to the ways of such technology, Bob attached his bunch of keys to the contraption and went to play for Evensong.

> "I started to play a prelude, and from the organ stool came loud chirps as the key finder responded to my call — on the organ. I had to fumble around, extract the wretched thing and bury it under a few layers of cushions which fortunately were handy. It chirped throughout the service while the organ was playing, but the sound was subdued by the wad of cushions. I do not know where the device is now, but I detached my keys and left the thing at home from that time on."

Beauty is in the ear of the beholder when evaluating volume. Some listeners positively vibrate in ecstatic sympathy when every available 16ft and 32ft pipe is in action. Or worse. Keith John went to a concert in the Eglise de Chant d'Oiseau in Brussels. The combination of instruments was organ, plus 16 (or thereabouts) hunting horns. "It was the most extraordinary and peculiarly impressive sound I have ever heard and, in that vast acoustic, absolutely deafening."

When Liverpool Cathedral organ was under construction, initial voicing was done in the Willis Liverpool factory, causing some unhappiness in a neighbouring school. The tuba speaks on 50-inch wind and is an immensely powerful stop. While it was on the voicing machine, a fault developed in the specially contrived temporary action and all 61 notes on the tuba ciphered at the same time. The result was said to be indescribable.

For many years movable consoles have been found in churches and concert halls that present frequent organ recitals. Without doubt the crowds are bigger and the interest higher because the audience can watch the organist perform. On more than one occasion Fred Swann has found a console moving away from him because it had not been properly anchored.

At the other end of the performance spectrum, anyone who has pumped an old-fashioned country church harmonium through all 12 verses of *Lift High the Cross* will have found their stool moving more or less to the next aisle in the course of playing it. I got wise to this, and always stationed a hefty minder with whopping size 11 shoes planted at one corner of the stool.

The more permanent variety of console is kitted out as a home away from home. Organists report that treasures found at the console or close to hand in the loft have included peppermints, dentures, tatty old music, suitcases, a set of golf clubs, broken pencils, cream for piles, and once a carefully garnered heap of takeaway menus. A telephone at the console is almost essential, especially during the Rugby World Cup. When New Zealand-born Katherine Dienes-Williams was at Liverpool Metropolitan Cathedral, she stationed a 'sick' chorister in an office so he could phone through the score from downstairs.

> "One such call came through during the Howells in B minor Magnificat. My organ scholar went to turn the page, but the phone light was flashing, indicating it was an incoming call. 'Never mind the page,' I said, 'just get the phone.' It was OK — the All Blacks won."

A source of constant fascination, to organists as well as the general public, stops and stop knobs are great when they work, and extremely scary when they do not. As moving parts, the potential for thrills and spills is omnipresent. If they should be out, they stay stubbornly retracted; if they should be in, they tap dance over *ppp* passages.

Sometimes stops part company with the organist and console entirely. At Winchester Cathedral, James Lancelot was accompanying Gibbons' Second Service and reached for the Choir Piccolo. Out it came, all two feet of it, just as the stop knob said. He was able to keep playing with one hand and both feet while he manoeuvred the stop-rod back into place with the other hand. Things could have been worse, he said. "I was glad it had not been the Double Open Wood 32ft; I could not have coped with that length of stop knob".

During David Briggs's time as a layclerk at Ely Cathedral, Arthur Wills nearly always accompanied the psalms. His choice of organ stops, as well as additional effects, was inspirational and occasionally amusing. David remembers his not-so-subtle inclusion of a low pedal glissando during the verse of Psalm 73 — '*Nevertheless my feet were almost gone: and my steps had well-nigh slipped*'. It was also reported that, on one particularly stormy night during Evensong, the choir was singing Psalm 78. At the verse '*He loosed upon them the furiousness of his wrath, anger, displeasure and trouble*' there was a loud clap of thunder, which shook the building. After the service, one of the layclerks called across the vestry "Was that a new organ stop, Arthur?"

The evocative names for stops can be studied in their own right.[17] According to David Rumsey, the famous organ builder, P. G. Andersen (of *Organ Building and Design* fame) perpetuated his initials (which also gave him the local nickname of P.G.) in the Pegal stop on the Lund Cathedral choir organ. It is a Regal, but the name is not a misprint.

A few old German organs sport a jolly stop called a Fuchsschwanz. The name comes from the German "fuchs" (fox), "schwanz" (tail), and "schwank" (joke). The knob was not inscribed with its name, but occasionally a sign "Noli me tangere" ("Do not touch") was attached to the console. People whose curiosity did get the better of them and dared touch the knob would set free the catch of a spring, causing a huge foxtail to fly out into their faces. Sometimes the foxtail was simply attached to the stop knob. Having drawn the tail out of the jamb, it is difficult to replace it; some claim that a builder is needed to put it back in place.

Modern organs are not to be left out of these in-jokes. In addition to Rieger's cocktail cabinet stops at Ratzeburg Cathedral (see page 167), Klais Orgelbau in Germany made sure they put a 64ft Vox Balaena (which translates as Voice of a whale) in their 2006 installation in the First United Methodist Church, Richardson. What is also on the same console, but not listed on the specification, is a stop labelled Texas that automatically plays *The Eyes of Texas* when drawn. Barry Jordan says that if you draw the Vox Strigis (Stimme der Eule — sound of the owl) stop on the organ of St Sebastian's Cathedral in Magdeburg, a wooden owl appears from the side of the Rückpositif case and says 'Hooo' rather plaintively.

17 See Ed Stauff's unique website devoted to organ stops at www.organstops.org

Organ builders and tuners

"Think yourself lucky you don't have to crawl around in it!"

Often forgotten about until something goes wrong, the organ tuner/builder who installs or maintains the organ is as important as the person playing it. Inaugural recitals are the first public outing of their workmanship, and the builder is easily spotted as the fingernail-chewing, brow-mopping wreck pacing between loft and nave. James Lancelot recognises this well:

> "Organ builders are always understandably nervous at opening recitals; and they do not like long held notes, regarding them as tempting fate. Occasionally the two shibboleths march hand-in-hand. Harrison and Harrison rebuilt the organ in Västerås Cathedral, Sweden magnificently in the 1990s, and along with Marie-Claire Alain and the resident organist, Mats Ericson, I participated in the opening ceremony.
>
> I was sitting in the loft with one of Harrison and Harrison's builders while Mats was playing a little-known work by his predecessor, Hugo Melin. In one movement, there was an exceptionally long held note — minutes rather than seconds in length. Eventually it ceased and the music moved on; only then did I dare to look at my

> neighbour. Ashen-faced, he reciprocated; the look in his eyes said it all."

Sometimes the anxiety is justified. John Wells recalls the opening of a new organ in Vermont when he was studying in Indiana.

> "A cipher was a little embarrassing but quickly fixed. A broken tracker then occurred but was still repaired in reasonable time. When a coupler seriously malfunctioned (it was a mechanical action), I could see the builder's face complete its descent from joyful expectation to concern, then down to utter despair. We took the interval there. I think we finished the concert somehow but have blanked that part from my memory. I suppose the builder probably did the same."

Awkward moments appear when you least expect them; an organ consultant told the story of a young organ tuner who, just before a concert, accidentally stood on a couple of small pipes. He decided to hide them in the toilet cistern pending removal at a later and at a less public moment. The distinguished visiting organist arrived and paused, just before entering the building, to acknowledge a greeting from a group of admirers. At that moment a cascade of water spouted from the upper level soaking both him and the music in his hand. The pipes had jammed the floating ballcock in the tank, and the water had poured out of the overflow pipe. It is not recorded what happened when it was discovered that parts from a rank of pipes from the main organ were being stored in a lavatory cistern.

Despite relatively minor hiccoughs, for centuries builders have been sufficiently proud to sign their names and leave other doodlings on the organ case; latterly they add thumbnail photos of themselves alongside their signatures. The graffiti varies. A one-time tuner and maintenance man for Hill, Norman and Beard, used to work on a small organ near Basingstoke. He always puzzled over a series of numbers written inside the swell box. Then it dawned on him: because the Swell was the last division to be tuned, it showed the times of return railway trains from the station to London.

Organ graffiti fascinated David King, who worked for nearly two years as an organ builder for Czelusniak et Dugal in Northampton.

> "Besides getting the usual calls from clueless clergy ('The organist says one of the keys is sticking. I think it was D minor.') I also experienced the time-capsule aspect of pipe organs: organ graffiti. Scratched in the wall of the chamber of an old Hook and Hastings in Chicopee were the words 'Orgun Gang, 1938', clearly the result of a group of Sunday School students who had watched too many Bowery Boys movies.
>
> Aeolean-Skinner employees tended to use the insides of their wind chests for scrap paper, scribbling calculations on whatever chunk of wood was handy. It was clear from Opus 857 (1931) in Holyoke, MA, that they were a bit mathematically challenged. Besides the basic calculations written out in full ('20 + 30 = 50,' '35 / 7 = 5') my favourite was '17 x 6 = 102 + 13 = 125.' This was on the inside of one rung of a ladder leading up to the swell chamber. Bill Czelusniak took one look at it and said, 'Well, no wonder that ladder was so long.'
>
> Then there were the horror stories we were called in to repair: a 16ft pedal rank 'racked' by being tied off to a raw 2x4 with nylon clothes line, or the radically rescaled flute rank with new upper lips made out of aluminum roof flashing, or the tuning slides made of electrical tape. It is astonishing what some builders have put in their instruments. A fair amount of the work by Czelusniak et Dugal was undoing the damage done by other builders."

Some builders were only too happy to lend a hand, especially if it helped make a point. English organ builder, Noel Mander, had gone to Manchester by train to see a job in Stockport, but he missed his return train:[18]

> "To kill time, I went in to look at the cathedral. Harrison's men were at work on it, and the foreman was a very good chap called Jack Hindle. I walked up and had a look.
>
> "Interested?" they asked. I said yes.
>
> "You an organ builder?" I said I was.
>
> "Who do you work for?" I said Mander.
>
> "God, he's a bastard, isn't he?"was the reply. Noel did not let on then who he was. But some years afterwards:
>
> ". . . they were working at the Temple, and they dropped two pipes, damaging them quite badly. They were terrified of sending them back to Durham, so brought them along to us to repair. Wally Thacker came in and said 'Harrison's men are outside and want us to repair a pipe or two they've broken.'
>
> I said, "Of course we will — repair them while they wait."

In due course, Thacker came back and said, "They want to know how much we'll charge them."

> "Tell them the old bastard won't charge them anything."

Not all difficulties with organs arise from the instruments: the owners are part of the problem. Noel Mander's daughter, Polly, tells of the time her father was examining the organ in Blenheim

18 "*Fanfare for an Organ Builder*" Postif Press

Palace. He arrived to find the Duke of Marlborough repairing an organ roll with sticky tape.

> "Horrified, he said, 'I cannot stand by and watch you do that! The roll is a unique record and you are damaging it.' The Duke replied he could not let my father speak to him in this way, in his own home. My father lost the job. He would not mince his words for anyone when a precious artefact was at stake."

Tuning log books, where the organist notes any problems with the organ for the tuner or builder to correct, are a vehicle for some to vent frustration, humour, or despair. Colin Mitchell recalls a tuning book in which was written in large red letters, by (presumably) a visiting organist:

> "This organ is the biggest load of **** I have ever played upon."

He showed this to the tuner, who wrote underneath in blue:

> "Think yourself lucky you don't have to crawl around in it!"

Animals

Cats — great and small

"A fat black cat, stared at me. A few seconds later, this cheeky creature jumped on the pedal board."

In the late 1960s David Rumsey began to think the laws of physics had been changed without notice; tuning slides on an organ he played in Adelaide would move great distances down their pipes, quite irrationally, apparently of their own accord and certainly without human intervention.

> "We checked them repeatedly and were convinced they were all tight and could not slip of their own accord. Yet tuning was only stable during the daytime. The explanation came late one evening when, in the dead of night, needing to practise, I found my way into the darkened and quite spooky church. Switching on the console light, then the motor, I began to play. Immediately a white apparition shot through the façade pipes, jumped at me hissing, scrambled over my shoulder and disappeared into the dark. I just had time to recognise the rectory cat. Kitty was henceforth banned, even from

her hitherto customary liturgical visits on Sunday mornings."

Felines will investigate any cat-sized cavity, and often find themselves contributing, one way or another, to the 'kist o' whistles'. Roy Tankersley noticed the family cat taking an unusual interest in the pedal board area of his house organ. Accustomed to the bizarre ways of felines, he dismissed it until he tried to demonstrate the organ to a visitor.

> "I began to play a few extracts, but in the lower half of the pedal board the notes seemed to hang on — for the first time I had ciphers. I apologised and quickly removed the lower panel to see what was wrong. Behind the action there was a dark mound, and two eyes looking up at me. A strange cat was wedged tightly inside. The pedal board was removed and the parts dismantled around the terrified cat. Once the action had been moved, the cat was free to leave and finally coaxed out by food, milk, and pleading family members. She (or he) seemed none the worse for the experience, and once a little food was consumed, soon escaped over the garden wall."

The organ in St Andrew's Cathedral in Honolulu, Hawaii, is in the chancel, on both sides above the choir stalls, with the console placed on the ground floor. Temperatures in Hawaii are hot and humid all year, and since few churches have air conditioning, doors and windows of the sanctuary are left wide open during services and recitals. Hans Hielscher was playing a soft cantabile during a recital in St Andrew's when, out of the corner of his eye, he saw something black moving towards the console.

> "A fat black cat, stared at me. A few seconds later, this cheeky creature jumped on the pedal board, (maybe she had discovered a mouse somewhere)? I tried to push her from the pedal board with my left foot or right foot, depending on which one was not engaged for the Can-

> tabile at the time. Finally, I got her, and with a yowl, she pushed off. Nobody in the audience realised what had happened at the console which at that time was hidden in the choir stalls (today it stands on a movable platform), except maybe for seeing a cat disappear in a flash."

Animal-loving Fred Swann is frequently stalked by feline fans. During his 18 years as Director of Music and Organist at the famed Crystal Cathedral Fred played the organ for literally hundreds of performances of Christmas and Easter pageants. These were major productions with the finest sets, costumes, and lighting, and an animal contingent of nearly 100 in addition to the large human cast. Fred would often visit the 'zoo' area where the trained animals were quartered during the several weeks that the pageants ran.

> "I was particularly taken with a beautiful tiger 'kitten', Alicia, born during the run of one of the pageants. The man who trained the tigers helped me get accepted by Alicia's mother, who allowed me to pick Alicia up, scratch her stomach, and pet her (she weighed only 35 pounds then). We bonded that first year and in subsequent years we became good friends, and I frequently helped the trainer tend to Alicia's needs. One year, after she was grown, and weighed 350 pounds, she arrived at the cathedral for a run of *The Glory of Easter*.
>
> I was practising in the cathedral. Imagine my delight when Alicia poked her head round the console murmuring greetings. Tourists in the building were mesmerised, and did they get a treat! We had Alicia jump up on top of the console where she laid down, or stood up, all the time gazing fondly at me. A friend called the church photographer and a number of wonderful photos were taken. The tourists' cameras were going off constantly, and I have wondered how they explained those shots to their friends back home."

No one in a small town in Missouri will forget one of Fred's recitals on their home patch. He was playing Jean Langlais' quiet *Song of Peace* that was programmed before Langlais' *Cats*. Fred kept hearing a cat mewing.

> "Then, soon after I started *Cats*, a side panel on the console banged on the floor and a cat jumped out, ran a few feet, turned around and walked back near the console and told me off in fortissimo cat chatter. We surmised that the church cat had climbed into the console over the expression shoes. The tuner had left the screws out of the side panel in order to gain quick access to two knobs that had been sticking."

When Fred repeated a performance of *Cats* in Texas, the church cat walked in calmly from a side room, sat, looked at the audience, had a quick wash, and then ran off as Fred played the final two "scat" chords.

Dogged — by bats and birds

"I do not suppose that many members of my audience realised why the picture occasionally went berserk and fuzzy."

Dogs are usually far better behaved than cats. My tri-colour sheepdog (who had voting rights at the New Zealand General Assembly) was raised from puppyhood to sleep on the organ bench, moving later to beside the pedals when she grew too big, eventually becoming a member of the small church choir. With her alongside me at the organ, unsavoury characters approaching the console backed off when my Bach was replaced by her woof. We were constant companions, so when I spent 10 weeks in hospital we pined for each other. Someone suggested playing a tape of 'her' organ as a consolation, but it made her more unhappy. Each time she would circle the speakers, unable to find the organ, or me, then sit back on her haunches and howl until it was turned off. What a fan.

David Aprahamian Liddle's guide dog, Crane, also behaved impeccably and was a seasoned champion of the art of concert kipping. At Gloucester Cathedral, the audience could watch David playing, thanks to closed circuit television. Crane, recognising another long spell of sleep time approaching, curled up underneath the CCTV camera tripod.

> "Anyone who knows dogs will have observed how every now and then they get up, twirl around a few times, then slump down and snooze again. I don't suppose that many members of my audience realised why the picture occasionally went berserk and fuzzy."

There can be nothing so nerve-racking as trying to make an organ recording under pressure of time yet being constantly interrupted. It is possible to remain relatively calm despite with the usual background noise of aircraft, motorbikes, bells, recalcitrant youths yoboing around outside the West Door, itinerant priests wandering past rattling their keys, and so on, but what about stray animals? More specifically, what is the solution to an air force of winged creatures? Graham Barber learned the hard way what to do when a session grinds to a halt because bats are dive-bombing the microphones:

> "This happened one night in Lincoln Cathedral during a recording of English Romantic music on the wonderful Willis organ there. The mood swung from mild amusement to increasing irritation, and subsequently to a torrent of expletives which made the stone effigies blush. Then the ever-resourceful Andrew Parker started a bit of lateral thinking. It went as follows: 'The bats have come out because they think it is night-time. We need to persuade them that it is not night-time but daytime. Solution: switch all the lights on.' Once this was done, the bats went back to their perches and fell fast asleep again, basking in the full glare of the nave lights."

During another recording, Graham then had to solve the problem of how to free a cheerfully chirping, but increasingly agitated bird that was trapped in the church.

> "At St Bartholomew's, Armley, during the day, a trapped bird grew weaker but its chirps grew ever stronger and more piercing. We opened as many doors as we could, but when we tried to chase it out, it simply

> flew to another part of the building. Then we noticed that it kept alighting on a vase of flowers and pecking them, presumably because it was thirsty. Neil Collier, mastermind of Priory Records, hit on the solution. He moved the flowers to a position near the open doors. When the bird once again came down to quench its thirst he was able to chase it out through the South Porch."

Paul Jacobs had a creature a little more aggressive than birds and bats to contend with when he performed in Houston, Texas. The programme included several pieces of Messiaen, one of which was the ethereal *Desseins éternels* from *La Nativité*.

> "For the concert, the console was moved to the front and centre, in full view of the audience, so I took extra care that all body language should be complementary to the spirit of the music, never distracting from it. With such a blissfully profound piece as *Desseins éternels*, I found myself in a serene, almost trance-like state.
>
> In my peripheral vision I saw what appeared to be a pesky fly buzzing about the pedal board. Attempting to ignore it, I continued this glorious music, which magically seemed to make time stand still. While holding the final pianissimo chord, I noticed it was not an innocuous little fly which came to rest on my right knee, but rather an insect far more intimidating: a jumbo red wasp! Taking great care not to upset the nasty insect, I did not move a muscle until having released the last celestial chord, when I simultaneously rocketed off the organ bench. The wasp, fortunately, did not inject its stinger into my knee, but chose instead to fly off. The audience wondered why I so abruptly darted from the bench. I explained, which they seemed to find amusing. Audiences do love it when things go wrong."

Two Personal views

Triumphs and tribulations of an organ tuner's life

(written for the Northern Cathedrals Festival brochure in the late 1990s)

by Mark Venning

Visitors to churches and cathedrals will occasionally be surprised, alarmed or affronted by curious semi-musical noises emanating from transept or triforium. Those who listen more carefully will recognise the unmistakable sound, all too familiar to vergers and other nature-lovers, of the organ tuner calling to his mate. Shy and retiring by nature, he is one of the unsung heroes of the world of church music. The organ is the largest and most complex of all musical instruments, and the tuner needs to be a highly-skilled technician with a keen musical ear. He can make all the difference to an organ's health and happiness. Quite often, he can prevent a catastrophe; in small ways, by curtailing the activities of woodworm and field-mice, or sometimes on a larger scale.

When our tuner visited a famous chapel in Nottinghamshire a few years ago, he observed a crack in the floor, concealed within the organ, which had not been there on his previous visit. He reported this to the owners, just in time to avert the complete collapse of the building due to mining subsidence. Multi-million-pound repairs have only recently been completed.

More often, of course, it is necessary to deal with disasters after the event, and most tuners have a rich store of such experiences. Water is a common cause of fun. I well remember receiving an eyeful from the front pipes of a village organ while investigating a report of mysterious gurgles from the Open Diapason — the organ had literally filled up with water from a hole in the roof. More spectacularly, the ringers at a Bristol church left the bells 'up' overnight a few months ago. It rained, perhaps unusually hard; the bells filled up with water; and on Sunday morning when the bells were 'pulled off', ringers and organ received a 10-bell soaking. Even more recently, a school swimming bath was due for maintenance: the water was drained but, unfortunately, the wrong tap was turned and the entire contents emerged in the Chapel, flooding the organ to a depth of several feet.

Water may be unwelcome in organs, but wind is essential. Sadly, few organs now are blown by hand. Human blowers were often ripe and simple characters, about whom a rich fund of stories developed ("It takes 396 pumps for the Hallelujah Chorus, and I don't care if you haven't finished"). Water-powered blowing came next, as recalled in an enchanting series of letters to *The Times* a year or two ago, including one from James Lancelot about being forbidden to take a bath during matins because the resulting drop in water pressure would cause the organ to wail into ignominious silence. Oil and steam engines have also been tried. The organist of one of our country churches was killed when he became entangled in the machinery. Another fuel was gas, the fumes of which ruined many an organ before it was phased out.

Today, most organs are blown less erratically by electric fans. The Royal Albert Hall has 56 horsepower. The equipment in Peterborough Cathedral is underground in the churchyard, and strong men turn pale when a tombstone rises and the ghastly figure of an organ builder is silhouetted against the darkening sky. At Peterborough, too, a 19th-century candlestick recently jammed inside an obscure part of the wind system, causing an embarrassing wind shortage. It must have been lying there innocently since 1894. The sub-organist pointed out anxiously that candlesticks usually come in pairs. At Ely, the main wind trunks run up the outside of the cathedral. One day they fractured near the triforium, causing an extremely rude and continuous noise which could be heard all over the city.

Some blowing faults are easy to cure. Not long ago, I received a bitter complaint that one of our organs was short of wind, so I made a long journey from Durham to investigate. The blower was in a hutch in the beer garden of the Choristers' Arms, next to the church. Amid ribald comments from the customers I inserted myself into the blowing chamber, to discover that the fan was running backwards after the church had been re-wired. The fault was solved, and the smell of alcohol in the organ area was at last satisfactorily explained.

Quite often creatures, alive or dead, need to be dealt with. Woodworm are an obvious threat. Moth eat felt, and mice eat leather. At Westminster Abbey the quality of the music was such that a mouse went into an ecstatic trance between the folds of the bellows, and awoke in heaven when the organist switched off the wind; his flattened skeleton was eventually found by Mr Harrison on a visit of inspection. Birds have an unhappy way of dying in organ pipes. One pigeon had lodged itself so firmly in the crook of a Trombone pipe that the tuner despaired of dislodging it. Eventually he had the bright idea of attaching a hose to the narrow end and turning the water full on; the bird, in a ripe state of decomposition, shot out and flew, faster in death than in life, straight into the path of the vicar, who needed re-voicing afterwards. Other similar stories are too gruesome to print.

Then there is the human element. Is the organ unaccountably silent? Thieves may have removed the pipes, or the lead from the roof. Is a note sticking? The organist may have dropped a hymnbook on the keys, or a pencil lead between them. Have the bellows jammed? The flower ladies may have put the Christmas crib, assorted vases, and the spare candlesticks in that useful cupboard just below the organ pipes. Canny workmen are a constant source of problems. Electricians fasten cables to moving parts, and a trailing flex is quite enough to knock over the smallest pipes, ready to be trampled on. Builders and decorators fill the organ with rubble, or drop bricks from a height. The permutations are unlimited.

Some episodes veer between fantasy and farce. A stained-glass expert arrived at a country church to examine a window behind the organ. He stood on a row of sixteen-foot pipes, which duly collapsed with a domino effect, bringing him with them. Thus brought low, he picked himself up and went off to the vicarage for a restorative cup of tea. When he returned with the vicar, the church was full of smoke — an electric cable had fractured and set fire to the bellows. The fire brigade brought the saga to a watery end, leaving the tuner to clear up.

Ciphers (unwanted notes, alternatively known in country districts as syphons) are the most conspicuous form of organic misbehaviour. Some are written in the music. Long pedal notes are always worrying for the organ builder, especially at opening recitals. Franck's *Prelude, Fugue and Variation* is notorious for bringing tuners out in nasty rashes. At the dedication of the Hereford Cathedral organ, the tuner dived in head-first to silence the offending note; in the ensuing race between him and Franck, the latter won by a semi-quaver.

Organists vary in their reactions to mechanical difficulties. The best of them sail serenely on through perils and disasters, modulating as necessary. I was called out one Saturday afternoon to a Cathedral. My small daughter (useful for reaching the parts most organ builders cannot reach) and I mended the cipher five minutes before a big service. We then sat inside the organ and watched through a chink in the wainscot while the Bishop, Chancellor, Dean and Canons entered in stately procession. The music sounded familiar. We soon recognised an eloquent arrangement of the organ builders' signature tune, *Oh dear, what can the matter be?*

In Tune

By Christopher Herrick

As the front man of organ concerts and recordings, I am gratefully aware of the huge debt we organists owe to the noble army of organ builders, technicians and tuners. On countless occasions these wonderful dedicated people have fine-tuned an organ for an event or sprung to the rescue when something has gone awry. Tuning and maintenance stories are legion.

For instance, two organ tuners were camped in the innards of the Royal Albert Hall organ during my Organ Prom in the 1990s. It was before the total rebuild of the instrument. I tell the truth when I say that I was really nervous before the concert, not so much about my playing as about the potential disaster due to the state of the instrument, which was terminally precarious. I got through the ordeal, buoyed up by the extraordinary atmospheric support of the Prom audience. In the event, the organ behaved quite well, hinting at giving up the ghost only twice. Phew!

Peter Batchelder and Doug Hunt are two of New York's finest organ technicians. Peter had the Alice Tully Hall organ in perfect tune for my *Complete Bach* series, 14 concerts in 14 days. He also gave generously of his time listening for hours to my preparation, advising me of the balance from the body of the hall, which I had no way of judging from the console. As he was a sensitive musician and good organist himself, I was more than pleased to accept his advice. Only a dedicated master of his craft could have kept that instrument, covered as it was by layers of dust and dirt, in such good shape for the series, and with so little time available to him.

Doug Hunt always managed to keep the giant St Bartholomew's organ with its far-flung divisions beautifully in tune. But there was the one awful occasion when I came the evening before a noon concert to prepare on a perfectly tuned organ. Snow was on the ground outside, but the building was comfortably heated. During the night there was a temperature swing from freezing to what in Britain would be a comfortable summer temperature. Unfortunately, the thermostat in the church had malfunctioned and the boilers continued to belch forth heat into the building. Doug woke in the middle of the night and with an extraordinary display of intuition and dedication to duty he went over to the church in the small hours and systematically retuned as much of the organ as he could. But even with this noble effort the organ still sounded more like a giant Wurlitzer than the glorious St Bart's organ at the concert.

Such temperature lurches can happen even where there are modern climate control systems such as in Dallas's Meyerson Symphony Hall. The brilliant Fisk organ was well tuned for my concert and should have been in fine shape for the *Organ Fireworks* recording that was timetabled after the weekend. We did not reckon on a concert by an ageing British pop star. He had complained that the hall temperature was too high, so the duty manager 'aired' it, with disastrous results for the organ tuning. The standby tuner found a much greater workload than any of us anticipated and a great deal of valuable time was wasted.

There are many occasions when self help is the only option in the absence of a professional organ technician. In fact, I often 'touch up' the reeds when necessary and desirable.

It had been agreed that the Rieger organ in Hong Kong's Cultural Centre was to be tuned ready for our recording. However, the tuner was apparently unable to be on standby. We arrived in the morning of our first recording day and the organ was in perfect condition except for one pipe, the middle F sharp on the swell 8' Trumpet, which was sounding C. After ascending numerous vertical ladders, opening and closing as many trapdoors, I arrived at the top of the organ inside the swell box to encounter a bunch of pipes, rather like a small field of tulips. Luckily the offending pipe was on the edge, otherwise the combination of 'notched' tuning springs with my lack of a reed knife would have been extremely challenging.

On another occasion, in Ottawa Cathedral, I did manage to summon up sufficient courage to climb one of these dreaded vertical ladders onto a rickety duckboard. When I got up there and realised the danger getting any nearer to the large pedal pipe that needed tweaking, I quickly descended to terra firma, having decided that an alive organist playing a concert with one out-of-tune pedal note was preferable to a dead organist and no concert.

Mistooks

"The typesetter had made a serious omission . . . "

Misprints in a hymn sheet or recital programme always liven proceedings. The bereaved family of a very rich man for whose funeral I played smiled along with the congregation when they came to a particular line in *Guide me, oh Thou Great Redeemer.* It was printed as "Land my safe on Canaan's Side". A misplaced advertisement can make curious bed-fellows. When in Sydney to give a concert Martin Setchell wondered why there was no sign of the event in the newspaper. The organisers were adamant: it had definitely been published. After many minutes of searching we found it all right — tucked cosily between the call girl and escort services of Sydney's nightlife.

No-one is exempt from typographical errors. Simon Preston sent his recital programme, which included Liszt's *Ad Nos,* for typing. The secretary called him back with a question about the Liszt. "Which numbers would you like me to add, Mr Preston?" Here are a few more goodies from the wondrous world of printing gremlins:

- James Welch submitted music for the bulletin, and the church secretary asked him how to spell Bach's name. He spelled "J. S. B. A. C. H." It appeared in the bulletin as "Jay S. Bach."

- A classical music download site listed the chorale prelude "*An Wasserflüssen Babylong*".

- It was stewardship Sunday and the offertory was listed as: *Jesus, Priceless Treasurer.*

- A church secretary once left the "i" out of a flyer advertising a concert: "Come to our Organ Rectal".

- During a communion service the organist played a chant which, according to the bulletin, the title was: *Adoro pee devote.*

- A church bulletin in Utica reported the organist would play *Plein Jell* by Clerambault.

- A church bulletin in Portland, ME, listed the prelude for the first Sunday of January as *The Old Year Now Is Pissed Away.*

- Publicity in a glossy UK organ magazine for a concert in 2007, in Victoria Hall, Hanley, Stoke-on-Trent, advertised the inclusion of "*Suite Boutique*" by Leon Boellmann.

- Michael Whitehall relates that a special service at Manchester Cathedral included Leonard Smith's 1974 song *Our God Reigns.* The refrain ("Our God reigns! Our God reigns! Our God reigns! Our God reigns!") was printed after each verse — almost. Light relief from such tedious repetition was afforded by a misprinted final refrain ending "Our God resigns!"

- Geoffrey Atkinson gave his choir the Peter Cornelius' *Three Kings* to sing on Epiphany. The text printed in the order of service read: ". . . Shall lead thy heart to its resting place. Gold, incest, myrrh thou canst not bring. . ."

- Gerry Manning was asked by a wedding couple (in writing) for *The Cannon* by Paco Bell.

- Hats off to the over-active spellcheckers that, in at least three instances I have recorded, have turned *Satan* into *Santa.*

- The Easter church advertisements in the The Press, Christchurch, notified the faithful of a performance of Stainer's *Crucifixion* at St Barnabas, followed by the two-hour Good Friday vigil. The ad cheerfully also welcomed worshippers to "Hot-Cross Bums in the hall afterwards".

- Again, The Press advertised that "During Holy Communion service at 11am the preacher will be the Dead"

- Colin Mitchell and friends wanted to do their bit for an Royal Society for the Prevention of Cruelty to Animals service by choosing appropriate animal music for the voluntaries. So they had *The Swan* with cello and piano, the *Cuckoo* with the piano and the organ Claribel Flute, followed by *L'Eléphant* using piano and the 16ft pedal Ophicleide. A look at the *The Halifax Courier*, revealed the following: "6.30 pm Evensong (RSPCA Annual Service). Organ voluntaries: A selection from *Carnival* by Ste. Camille sans Animals."

- Amy Johansen used to play for a Baptist church in Pensacola, Florida. One Sunday she wanted to use the lively final section from the *Offertoire sur les grands Jeux* from a Couperin Mass for an exit voluntary. To avoid confusion with the offertory itself, she thought over the title while dictating the service list to the secretary on the phone. Finally she said, "let's call it Gigue . . . G.I.G.U.E." Amy helpfully spelled out the name. At the Sunday service the congregation was delighted to discover that the service would conclude with "*Let's call it Gigue*" by Francois Couperin.

Samuel Wesley wrote a few short music cameos that, due to their brevity, come under the enigmatic title *Scraps for Organ.* At the start of his career D'Arcy Trinkwon was invited to play in a beautiful village nestling high on the mountainous slopes around Lake Zurich. The small organ was charming, with a radiant, silvery sound that perfectly matched the picturesque surroundings. One of these *Scraps for Organ* would fit ideally into D'Arcy's programme as a musical sorbet between two bigger works.

> "When it came time for me to greet the audience, I was a little taken aback at the stifled giggling from various people, particularly from old school friends. Was it my outfit? (after all, I did have a lot fun dressing up for concerts when younger) Why were people sniggering so much?
>
> "As I stood in front of the audience, I looked at the programme in my hand. Somewhere in the printing process, the typesetter (this being just before computer technology was to sweep aside typeset programmes) had made a serious omission, and Samuel Wesley's *Scrap* was missing the crucial first letter. It appeared in the programme boldly as *A Crap for Organ*."

In his review of D'Arcy's concert, the critic wrote at length, extolling the beauty of the charming Crap by Samuel Wesley.

Pure Poetry

Oh Rancid Flaps of Ancient Suede

(Ode to my organ shoes)

Oh rancid flaps of ancient suede,
With groovèd soles and heels arrayed,
'Tis time to pen a eulogy
About your organ shoe-logy.

You've heeled and toed your fetid way
Through every piece I've dared to play,
With never a grumble, moan or whine
About a tricky fugal line.

Through hymns galore my feet have ploughed —
The bass part ringing clear and loud;
And with malodorous precision,
You have controlled my Swell division.

With registration too your part
You've played; and what a subtle art
It is, to cause the feet to jive
Between the pistons, one to five.

Attuned to Widor, used to Bach —
Through every age you've made your mark;
Chorale by Franck or one of Handel's —
You are no ordinary sandals.

You've been an aromatic play-link
Between the hands and feet in Sweelinck.
And though your age could well be Tudor
You've never shirked at Buxtehude.

You've danced through Brahms, you've flown through Liszt,
Of Mendelssohn you've got the gist:
And though you're old and worn and smelly —
You've Sortied out Lefébure-Wély.

Complete these praises now I must
To my old shoes, so rank, so just;
You have your eyes, your tongue, your sole, my dears —
It grieves me that you have no ears.

David Setchell (b. 1960) [19]

19 Winner of competition on subject of organ shoes, run by Dan Long on www.bachorgan.com

The Organ-Blower

DEVOUTEST of my Sunday friends,
The patient Organ-blower bends;
I see his figure sink and rise,
(Forgive me, Heaven, my wandering eyes!)
A moment lost, the next half seen,
His head above the scanty screen,
Still measuring out his deep salaams
Through quavering hymns and panting psalms.

No priest that prays in gilded stole,
To save a rich man's mortgaged soul;
No sister, fresh from holy vows,
So humbly stoops, so meekly bows;
His large obeisance puts to shame
The proudest genuflecting dame,
Whose Easter bonnet low descends
With all the grace devotion lends.

O brother with the supple spine,
How much we owe those bows of thine!
Without thine arm to lend the breeze,
How vain the finger on the keys!
Though all unmatched the player's skill,
Those thousand throats were dumb and still:

Another's art may shape the tone,
The breath that fills it is thine own.

Six days the silent Memnon waits
Behind his temple's folded gates;
But when the seventh day's sunshine falls
Through rainbowed windows on the walls,
He breathes, he sings, he shouts, he fills
The quivering air with rapturous thrills;
The roof resounds, the pillars shake,
And all the slumbering echoes wake!

The Preacher from the Bible-text
With weary words my soul has vexed
(Some stranger, fumbling far astray
To find the lesson for the day);
He tells us truths too plainly true,
And reads the service all askew, –
Why, why the – mischief – can't he look
Beforehand in the service-book?

But thou, with decent mien and face,
Art always ready in thy place;
Thy strenuous blast, whate'er the tune,
As steady as the strong monsoon;
Thy only dread a leathery creak,
Or small residual extra squeak,
To send along the shadowy aisles
A sunlit wave of dimpled smiles.

Not all the preaching, O my friend,
Comes from the church's pulpit end!
Not all that bend the knee and bow

Yield service half so true as thou!
One simple task performed aright,
With slender skill, but all thy might,
Where honest labor does its best,
And leaves the player all the rest.

This many-diapasoned maze,
Through which the breath of being strays,
Whose music makes our earth divine,
Has work for mortal hands like mine.
My duty lies before me. Lo,
The lever there! Take hold and blow!
And He whose hand is on the keys
Will play the tune as He shall please.

Oliver Wendell Holmes (1809 - 1894)

The Organ Blower II

Now I am a fellow of great versatility
I do odd jobs for the poor and nobility
Everyone calls me old General utility
Though to say what that means I have not the ability
One day I'm out with the squire shooting hare
Next I'm shoeing the parson's old mare,
'Cos first I do one thing and then do another
But there is one job I likes better than t'other

REFRAIN

When I blows the organ for our mister Morgan
Who plays at our church every Sunday so grand
The wind in the bellows makes music like cellos
And fiddles and trumpets, it's just like a band.
At weddings I pumps, while the other chap thumps
And the choir sings a hymn if they knows it
The organ's a treat, but without me it's beat
'Cos I am the fellow what blows it !

Last week in our village we had great hilarity
Round came a fair that won great popularity
They had an organ but without disparity
If you listened at all it was just out of charity

Still on the green every Jack with his Jill
Danced up and down with the most wonderful skill
But I thought it all looked a terrible tangle
And as for the music, 'twas naught but a jangle.

REFRAIN

When I blows the organ for our mister Morgan
Who plays at our church every Sunday so grand
The wind in the bellows makes music like cellos
And fiddles and trumpets it's just like a band
All hours of the day I'm a pumping away
It's a back-aching job and I knows it
But if I ever shirk, The old organ won't work
For I am the fellow what blows it.

Now times are changing, least that's what they say,
For things are all done in a new fangled way
And yesterday Vicar, he says to me Joe,
At the end of the year I'm a- feared you must go
I asked him what for, and he said with a sigh
'Cos the new organ's blowed by electricity
But pr'aps when I'm gone the folks will say NO
It don't sound the same now without poor old Joe

REFRAIN

But when I blows the organ for our mister Morgan
Who plays in our church every Sunday so grand
The wind in the bellows makes music like cellos
And fiddles and trumpets it's just like a band
But if there's a hitch in their switches and sich
Then the organ won't play and they knows it

So they'll say Come on Joe, Now just you have a go
'Cos I am the fellow, the stout hearted fellow
The long winded fellow what blows it !

(Author unknown)

Our Organ's Firm Foundations

(Sung to Aurelia, *The Church's One Foundation tune*):

1. Our organ's firm foundations are Diapasons fat.
Installed in 1920, from that day since, they've sat.
From builder famed we sought it —
the object of our pride.
For fifteen grand we bought it,
when our old tracker died.

2. Elect from every family of pipes that give a hoot,
its great specification: one reed, one string, one flute;
with leathered Diapasons
at sixteen, eight and four;
and sub and super couplers,
how could one ask for more?

3. Though with a scornful wonder men hear it sore oppressed,
by ciphers rent asunder, by windtrunk leaks distressed.

Yet choir boys are list'ning;
their cry goes up, "How long
before this hoot and hissing
cease drowning out our song?"

4. 'Mid toil and tribulation and heated vestry wars,
we wait the ruination of it forevermore;
till with some chiffing glorious
our longing ears are bless'd,
and leathered pipes notorious
shall be but scraps at rest.

5. Yet still we oil the swell shades each month with Three-in-One,
and grease the motor bearings, to quieten down its run;
O, mis'rable contraption!
Lord, grant us funds that we
might junk it for a tracker
with pressures less than three!

(author unknown; supplied by Joshua Anderson, Timaru, New Zealand.)

Contributors

Nearly all contributors have high academic qualifications, awards, titles, honorifics or other credentials. Apart from exceptional cases, in the interest of readability I have included only names, present appointments and/or interests if applicable. No offence or slight is intended. Websites and appointments were correct at the time of submission.

Robert **Ampt** has been the Sydney City Organist based at the Sydney town hall, Australia, since 1978 and is known as a composer and arranger of music. http://birralee.sydneyorgan.com/

Gail **Archer** is organist at Vassar College, Poughkeepsie, NY, USA, director of the music program at Barnard College, Columbia University, and a member of the organ and history faculty at the Manhattan School of Music in New York City. www.gailarcher.com

Geoffrey **Atkinson** has been Master of Music at Queen's Cross Church, Aberdeen, Scotland since 1977. A former music critic of the Aberdeen Press & Journal, he is prepared to wage war on ignorant clergy and stand up for established values. Frequently sober and not always as disgruntled as he looks.
www.Fagus-music.com (specialists in organ and choir music)

Philip **Bailey** is a former editor of The Organ Club Journal and a freelance church and concert organist based in West Sussex, UK

Graham **Barber** is an international concert organist and recording artist based in England. www.grahambarber.org.uk

Jennifer **Bate** is a British concert organist who gives master-classes worldwide and lectures on a wide range of musical subjects. Jennifer is regarded as a unique authority on the organ music of Messiaen. She was appointed OBE in 2008.
www.classical-artists.com/jbate/

Robert **Bates** is Professor of Organ at the Moores School of Music at the University of Houston, USA. He is an international recitalist and recording artist, composer, teacher, and author. He is currently writing a book on early French organs and registration practice.
http://www.music.uh.edu/people/bates.html

Kerry **Beaumont** has been the Director of Music at Coventry Cathedral in England since 2006, having served in a similar capacity at Ripon Cathedral (1994-2002) and St Davids Cathedral in Wales (1990-1994). www.kerrybeaumont.com

Tim **Bell** has played the pipe organ since he was 13 years old, originally at Nelson College and Nelson Cathedral, New Zealand.

Robert **Bowles** is a consulting structural engineer and a partner of Alan Baxter and Associates LLP, dealing mainly with historic stuctures. He is organist of the church of the Holy Spirit, Clapham, London, UK. His earliest experiences of church music were as a chorister of St Paul's Cathedral, London, England, where he now provides structural engineering advice.

David **Bridgeman-Sutton** has loved organs and organ music for more than 50 years. He has been fortunate in having jobs — and an understanding wife — that have allowed him to visit many instruments and to talk to organists, organ-builders and fellow enthusiasts in many countries. He has vivid memories of them all.
www.nzorgan.com

David **Briggs** is Director of Music at Aldeburgh Parish Church, England. Not to be confused with the concert organist, David Briggs, this David does not play the organ; he trains and directs the church choir, and promotes concerts in church. www.aldeburghparishchurch.org.uk

Gerard **Brooks** was recently appointed Director of Music at the Methodist Central Hall, Westminster, London, England after 20 years as Associate Director of Music at All Souls, Langham Place. www.gerardbrooks.org.uk

Paul **Carr** is Organist and Director of Music at St Paul's in the Jewellery Quarter, Birmingham, England, and a concert organist. www.paulcarr.co.uk/

Yves **Castagnet** has been titulaire organist for the choir organ of Notre-Dame de Paris since 1988. www.notredamedeparis.fr/Yves-CASTAGNET

David **Clark**, a New Zealand Presbyterian minister, values organists — organ voluntaries in his church are treated as worship, not cover for people entering or leaving. He believes in the 'real presence' of Christ in the sacrament of laughter, especially if it pricks clerical or musical pomposity. www.stlukes.org.nz

Peter **Clark** is organist and choirmaster at St Peter's Catholic Church, Cardiff, Wales. He lecturers in Theology and Religious Studies, specialising in Zoroastrianism; he watches too much Star Trek.

Julian **Cooper** is Assistant Director of Music at the church of St Thomas-on-The Bourne, Farnham, England. www.jonathan-lane.org.uk/page3.html

Robert **Cundick** is Organist Emeritus of the Mormon Tabernacle in Salt Lake City, Utah, USA, and he is a composer. http://en.wikipedia.org/wiki/Robert_Cundick

Christopher **Dawes**, for 12 years organist and later music director at St James' Cathedral in Toronto, Canada, is now a freelance-writer, musician and minister based with his wife and three children in Georgetown, near Toronto. www.orgalt.com

Richard **Dawson** is organist at Emmanuel Parish Church, Bentley and Organ Scholar at Emmanuel Parish Church, Wylde Green, England.

Pamela **Decker** is Professor of Organ and Music Theory at The University of Arizona in Tucson, USA and is organist at Grace St Paul's Episcopal Church. www.web.cfa.arizona.edu/sites/pdecker/

Paul **Derrett** is an "un-reformed, seriously obsessive organ addict, a rescuer of lost organs and an enthusiastic player and recorder of overlooked repertoire. I love it all." www.paulderrett.piczo.com

Nina De **Sole** is organiste Titulaire of Notre-Dame-du-Saint-Rosaire, Sainte-Thérèse-de-l'Enfant-Jésus et Saints-Barnabé-et-Clément, in Montréal Canada. www.geocities.com/ninotchka26/

Joan **DeVee Dixon** tours the globe as a concert musician and teacher. When not playing for "Polka Masses" in her home state of Iowa, USA, she is likely to be riding her Trek Madonne bicycle (just like Lance but not as fast). www.joandeveedixon.com

Emma Lou **Diemer** is professor emeritus of composition at the University of California, USA, and has been an organist in various churches since the age of 13. She has many works for organ in a vast catalogue of works in many genres.
www.emmaloudiemermusic.com

Katherine **Dienes-Williams** is the Organist and Master of the Choristers at Guildford Cathedral, England, where she directs the boys and men of the Cathedral Choir, and accompanies the girls of the Cathedral Choir. http://en.wikipedia.org/wiki/Katherine_Dienes

Graham **Dukes** is a medical doctor, lawyer and author, and when he can, he plays the organ and drives steam locomotives (the two have something in common). He lives in Oslo, Norway.

Richard **Elliott** is Principal Organist for the Mormon Tabernacle Choir, Salt Lake City, Utah, USA.
www.mormontabernaclechoir.org

Robert (Bob) **Elms** is organist and choirmaster at Wesley Church Albany West Australia and part-time organist (Saturday night mass) at Holy Family Church, Albany.

Jess **Eschbach** is Professor of Organ and Chairman of the Division of Keyboard Studies at the University of North Texas. He is gradually returning to concertizing after almost a 10-year hiatus with focal dystonia. www.music.unt.edu/organ

Malcolm J. **Farr** has been organist at parishes in Sydney, Australia and Montreal, Canada in former years. His current work means he travels a lot, and he is no longer "titulaire" of anything but his home toaster, which is on its last legs.

Jeremy **Filsell** is a British concert pianist and organist, well-known for his association with the music of Marcel Dupré. He is currently Principal Organist at the Basilica of the National Shrine of the Immaculate Conception in Washington DC, USA.
www.jeremyfilsell.com/

Roger **Fisher** was organist and Director of Music at Chester Cathedral, England for 29 years, retiring in 1996 to pursue a career as solo organist and pianist. He is a recording artist and broadcaster, organ construction adviser, and was Features Editor of Organists' Review for seven years. www.rogerfisher.org.uk

Frank **Fowler** was for 48 years a professional organ builder in England, starting as an indentured Apprentice with Hill Norman & Beard in 1947, and appointed as their Managing Director in 1974.

Richard **Francis** was formerly Organist and Choirmaster at St Laurence's Parish Church, Ludlow, Shropshire, England. He is now a freelance composer and has recently moved into the Corve Dale area not far from Much Wenlock. www.francismusic.co.uk/

Faythe **Freese** is Associate Professor at the University of Alabama organ department, USA.
www.concertartistcooperative.com/freese.html

Daniel E. **Gawthrop** is a composer based in the USA.
www.DunstanHouse.com

Gerald **Gifford** was formerly a member of the Professorial staff of the Royal College of Music, London, and Fellow and Director of Studies in Music at Wolfson College Cambridge. He now pursues a freelance international career as an organ and harpsichord recitalist and recording artist. He is also Honorary Keeper of Music at The Fitzwilliam Museum, Cambridge, England.
www.geraldgifford.com

David **Harrison** is a retired schoolmaster. His FRCO is a fond memory as he dons boxing gloves and skis to play at his local parish church in Worcester, England.

Peter **Harty** is an organ lover who practises medicine in Christchurch, New Zealand. He wants to maintain the pipe organ as an alive, wonderful, musical instrument that is available to all to discover, hear and enjoy, and not to be allowed to become extinct.

Bob **Heard** is a non-playing organ lover, who, during the 1970s shared his and his wife Pam's home in Gloucestershire, England with the ex-Ritz Cinema Hereford Compton organ, designed by Harold Ramsay. The stars came several times a year and played to audiences of 50.

Felix **Hell** has been a liturgical organist since the age of eight, and has given concerts in Germany and abroad since the age of nine.

He has performed more than 550 recitals in his native Germany, as well as abroad. www.felix-hell.com/

Christopher **Herrick** is an international concert organist who has devoted himself entirely to performance in recital, recording, and broadcasting. He performs regularly both as a soloist and with orchestras throughout the world. Christopher's collaboration with Hyperion since 1984 has produced almost 40 discs. www.christopherherrick.org

Hans Uwe **Hielscher** has been the organist and carilloneur at the Marktkirche in Wiesbaden, Germany, since 1979. In 1985 he worked at the Immanuel Presbyterian Church in Los Angeles, USA and he has been teaching at the University of Redlands in California since 1986. Hans has played more than 2,500 organ concerts worldwide. www.hielscher-music.de/

Peter **Hurford,** former organist of St Albans Cathedral for 20 years is an international recitalist, recording artist, composer, teacher and author (*Making Music on the Organ*) based in the UK. He is renowned for his interpretation of Bach and also for his influence as a teacher and was appointed OBE. http://www.bach-cantatas.com/Bio/Hurford-Peter.htm

Paul **Jacobs** is Chair, Organ Department, The Juilliard School, New York City, USA. www.concertartists.com/PJ.html

Amy **Johansen** is the Sydney University Organist, Australia and a recitalist and accompanist. www.usyd.edu.au/organ/organist.shtml

Keith **John** is a freelancing concert organist and pianist. www.hyperion-records.co.uk/a.asp?a=A98

Barry **Jordan**, born in South Africa, has been Director of Music at the cathedral in Magdeburg, Germany, since 1994. www.barryjordan.de

Russell **Kent** is a former Head of Music at Middleton Grange School in Christchurch and Music Adviser at the Department of Education for Canterbury and Westland, New Zealand. He freelances as relief organist for city churches and is organ tutor at two city schools.

David **King**: After achieving his BA in Philosophy, David had a checkered employment history that has left him able to tune a pipe organ, code a website, run a chain saw or rebuild a mass spectrometer. Twenty years ago, he took up his current day job as an independent book editor. www.davekingedits.com.

Michael **Koller** lives in the state of Washington in the USA with his wife Lorinda, daughter Alisa, Simon the cat and Kona the dog. He is a manager with the Farmers Insurance Group, and in his spare time presides over a 47-stop Rieger organ at the Sunnyside Seventh Day Adventist Church.

Roman **Krasnovsky**, born in the Ukraine, is an international concert organist, recording artist, and composer, based in Carmiel, Israel. http://www.organfocus.com/members/krasnovsky/

James **Lancelot** is Master of the Choristers and Organist of Durham Cathedral, England.
www.duresme.org.uk/CATH/organist.htm

Marie-Louise **Langlais** is professor for organ and improvisation at the Paris Conservatoire National de Région, France and is the widow of composer and organist Jean Langlais.
www.jeanlanglais.com

Douglas **Lawrence** is Director of Music at the Scots Church, Melbourne and Director of the Australian Chamber Choir. As a concert organist and conductor, he gives concerts every year in Australia and Europe. He has given about 80 performances of new Australian works and released 40 LPs or CDs.
www.douglaslawrence.org

David Aprahamian **Liddle** is a concert organist and composer, and organist of St Barnabas Pimlico, London, England. www.davidliddle.org

Dan **Long** launched the BACHorgan.com website in May 2001 to build a community of people who love the organ music of Johann Sebastian Bach. www.BACHorgan.com

John **Longhurst** was an organist for 30 years at the Mormon Tabernacle, in Salt Lake City, Utah, USA. http://en.wikipedia.org/wiki/John_Longhurst

Andrew **Lumsden** was sub-organist at Westminster Abbey and Organist at Lichfield Cathedral before being appointed Organist and Director of Music at Winchester Cathedral, England. He makes frequent broadcasts and tours abroad.

David **MacFarlane** is the full-time Director of Music at All Saints' Anglican Church, East St Kilda, Melbourne, Australia. He is an active recitalist on organ and harpsichord and is one of Australia's leading trainers of children's voices.

John **Mander,** (son of Noel Mander) is the managing director of the family firm Mander Organs based in London, England. www.mander-organs.com/

Polly **Mander,** (daughter of Noel Mander) is an Independent Scholar. Her subject area is musical reference in the works of Milton and Dante.

Gerry **Manning** has been Director of Music and Organist for 20 years at St George's Church, Guelph, Ontario, Canada. He is also a Professor Emeritus of English at the University of Guelph

Kimberly **Marshall** is Director of the School of Music at Arizona State University, USA, and the Patricia and Leonard Goldman Professor of Organ. www.music.asu.edu/organ

John **Maslen** is Organist at St. Peter's Church, Lawrence Weston, Bristol, and Reader at the same church. He was an organ builder for about eight years, but for the past 35 years has worked in the retail trade.

Marilyn **Mason** is Professor and Chair of Organ and University Organist at the University of Michigan, USA.
www.music.umich.edu/faculty_staff/mason.marilyn.lasso

Roy **Massey** is Organist Emeritus of Hereford Cathedral, England, and a past President of the Royal College of Organists.
http://www.herefordcathedral.org/music_organists_previous.asp

Frank **Mento** has been Titular Organist at Saint-Jean de Montmartre Church in Paris, France since 1979, and Professor of Harpsichord at the Conservatory of the 18th precinct in Paris since 1997.

Colin **Mitchell** is a music-graduate and former university organ-scholar, who fled professional music to pursue a career in finance and law in the City of London. Now a refugee in his native Yorkshire, his interests include music, writing and driving very large trucks. He has completed a novel entitled *The Mark of the Crystal.*

Alan **Morrison** is Organ Professor at the Curtis Institute of Music, the College Organist, Ursinus College, and Organ Professor at Westminster Choir College of Rider University, USA.
www.alanmorrison.us

Mary **Mozelle** is the Assistant Director of Worship and Music and Associate Organist at The Falls Church in the city of Falls Church, Virginia, USA. www.PipeOrganPro.com

June **Nixon** is Organist and Director of the Choir at St Paul's Cathedral, Melbourne, Australia. www.junenixon.com

Massimo **Nosetti** is an international concert organist based in Turin, Italy, where he is the cathedral organist. www.massimonosetti.it/

Nigel **Ogden** is presenter of BBC Radio 2 *The Organist Entertains* and is a concert organist whose performances link the often "ne'er the twain shall meet" worlds of the theatre and classical organ. www.bbc.co.uk/radio2

Gareth **Perkins** is a musician, organist, choir trainer and teacher, and organist at Paignton Parish Church, England. www.garethperkins.com

Edward D. **Peterson** has been Director of music and Organist at churches in Wisconsin, California, Pennsylvania in the USA; Lima (Peru) and in Puerto Rico, where he also taught organ students at the Pablo Casals Consevatory of Music. He lives in Clearwater, Florida, USA where he continues to coach organ and piano students, and transcribe music for the organ.

David **Pitches** is a medical doctor who is currently working for a charity in central Africa (Democratic Republic of Congo). www.medair.org

Mark **Quarmby** is Assistant Organist of St Andrew's Cathedral, Sydney, Australia; and a past President of The Organ Music Society of Sydney. www.mq.sydneyorgan.com

Raúl Prieto **Ramirez** is a concert organist and organist-in-residence at the modern National Concert Hall in Madrid, Spain. www.raulprieto.net

Cherry **Rhodes** is Adjunct Professor of Music at the Thornton School of Music, University of Southern California, Los Angeles, USA. www.usc.edu/schools/music/ private/faculty/cherryrh.php

David **Rothe** is Music Professor and University Organist Emeritus at California State University, Chico, USA. A recitalist and composer, David is also founder of the Chico Bach Festival, and Organist-Choirmaster at St Augustine's Anglican Church, Chico, CA. www.csuchico.edu/mus/organ/organs.htm

David **Rumsey**, born in Australia, has lived in Switzerland since the early 2000s, and pursues an international career in playing and consulting. His CV — in English, French or German — and selected articles he has written, can be found at www.davidrumsey.ch

David **Sadler** is a freelance musician, lecturer and writer living in Canterbury, New Zealand.

David **Sanger** is an organ recitalist and recording artist. He is also a well-known teacher, composer, editor and organ consultant. www.davidsanger.co.uk

John **Sayer** is an amateur organist who struggles to play all the right notes in the right order, who has been privileged to visit many of the great organs around the world and hear them played by those with no such limitations.

John **Scott Whiteley** is organist at York Minster, England. http://www.yorkminster.org/worship/music/the-organists/

David **Setchell** was formerly organist and choirmaster at St Ives Free Church and Bunyan Meeting, Bedford (and a schoolmaster in his spare time). He is now an itinerant pianist and piano tutor. Married with two children, he lives partially on his wits, partially on his allotment. www.dizzyfingers.co.uk

Martin **Setchell** is an international concert organist, Associate Professor of Music at the University of Canterbury, and organist at the Town Hall, Christchurch, New Zealand. He enjoys train travel, cricket and not mowing the lawn. www.organist.co.nz

William **Sharrow** was for 22 years Liturgist, Director of Music, and Organist at St Thomas Episcopal Church in St Petersburg, Florida, USA, where he "reined" over numerous adult choirs, organists, bride's mothers, and children's choirs. Although he has no children of his own, he has raised everyone else's.

Neil **Shepherd** is Director of Music, Standish Parish Church, Lancashire, England, and a music teacher, theatre organist, choral workshop and repertoire promotion and specialist music tours for choirs. www.neilshepherd.org.uk

Neil **Shilton** is a member of the Society of Organists Victoria, Australia and has been an organist in UK and Australia for 60 years.

Jason **Smart** was Organ Scholar at St George's Chapel, Windsor Castle under Dr Sidney Campbell from 1969 to 1972. He has been a frequent guest organist to the Rochester Cathedral Special Choir and currently freelances in the Plymouth area in England.

Philip **Smith** was Director of Music at The Collegiate Church of St Peter in Ruthin, Wales, where he was responsible for the installation of the 4-manual mechanical Willis organ. In 2008 he moved (with his cat Albert) to be organist of Auckland Cathedral, New Zealand. http://www.holy-trinity.org.nz/423.php

Ed **Stauff** is a software engineer by trade and a musician by calling. He plays more instruments than he has time to practice properly, but classical organ remains his first love. He currently serves as music director at an Episcopal church in northeast Massachusetts, USA. www.mewsic.com/Ed

Frederick (Fred) **Swann** is Organist Emeritus, Riverside Church, New York, The Crystal Cathedral (Garden Grove, CA), First Congregational Church of Los Angeles. Artist in Residence, St Margaret's Episcopal Church, Palm Desert, CA; University Organist and Professor of Organ, University of Redlands, CA, and President

of the AGO (2002-2008).
http://en.wikipedia.org/wiki/Frederick_Swann

Rick **Taft** has divided his free time between (among other things) music, cooking, history, beer brewing, go kart racing, beer drinking and sculpture, in ever-changing order of importance.
http://web.me.com/pipedreams/Pipe_Dreams/Welcome.html

Raphaël **Tambyeff** is Organist Emeritus at Notre Dame de Grâce de Passy Church in Paris, France.

Roy **Tankersley** is a free-lance organist, harpsichordist and choral director based in Palmerston North, New Zealand. He is musical Director of the Parish of St Marks and St Andrews in the City and the Schola Sacra Choir of Wanganui.

Adrian **Taylor** is organist at St John the Baptist, Boldre, Hampshire, England and director of the chamber choir Lauda.
www.adriantaylor.co.uk

Timothy **Tikker** is organist at St Thomas the Apostle Church, Ann Arbor, Michigan, and College Organist, Kalamazoo College USA.
http://ttikker.com

Richard **Townend**, a former pupil of Harold Darke, Frederick Sternfeld and Herbert Howells, is the resident recitalist at St Margaret Lothbury, London, England, where he has presented more than 1000 programmes on the 1801 George Pike England organ, once played by Mendelssohn. www.stml.org.uk/organ.html

Ian **Tracey** is the City of Liverpool Organist, Organist Titulaire of Liverpool Cathedral, Chorusmaster of the Royal Liverpool Philharmonic Society, Professor, Fellow and Organist at Liverpool John Moores University, England. http://www.itracey.org/

Ross **Trant**, from Canada, studied organ playing, design and construction in Toronto, Oxford and London. He is now retired. Learn a little more at: www.organfocus.com/members/r_trant/

D'Arcy **Trinkwon** is an international concert organist based in the United Kingdom. www.darcytrinkwon.com

Sean **Tucker** has been the Sub Organist of Wimborne Minster, England, since 1997. He also teaches at two schools and in private practice. He does not own a pet sheep and is pleased to say that he has never been to Chipping Sodbury. www.organanoraks.com/

Mark **Venning** is Managing Director of Harrison and Harrison Ltd, who have been building organs in Durham, England since 1872. www.harrison-organs.co.uk/

Gillian **Weir** is an internationally acclaimed concert organist performing worldwide at major festivals and with leading orchestras and conductors. A distinguished musician, she is known for her virtuosity and integrity, extending well beyond the world of the organ. Among her many awards and honours she was created DBE in 1996. www.gillianweir.com

James **Welch** is Organist at Santa Clara University, Santa Clara, California, USA. www.welchorganist.com

John **Wells** is Auckland City Organist, Organist to the University of Auckland, New Zealand, and erstwhile President of the NZ Association of Organists. He works as a freelance performer, composer and teacher. www.johnwells.co.nz/

Philip J **Wells** has a lifelong interest that focuses on the technical and historical aspects of pipe organ building. Much of his retirement in Gloucestershire, England, is devoted to data gathering for the UK National Pipe Organ Register. http://npor.emma.cam.ac.uk/

Michael **Whitehall** is a retired mathematician, organist at Hillington Parish Church, Norfolk, England (Snetzler 1756) and Secretary/Treasurer of the Incorporated Association of Organists Benevolent Fund.

Barry **Williams** wrote *Everything Else An Organist Should Know*. He is a lawyer and a musician, a Special Adviser to the Royal School of Church Music, Honorary Legal Adviser to the Cathedral Organists' Association and an Honorary Member of the Institute of British Organ building. www.organistpublications.co.uk/

David **Willcocks** , an ex-chorister of Westminster Abbey and organist of Salisbury Cathedral, Worcester Cathedral and King's College Cambridge, a universally renowned British choral conductor, organist, and composer. He was appointed CBE in 1971, received a knighthood in 1977 and has more than 50 honorary degrees. http://en.wikipedia.org/wiki/David_Willcocks

Arthur **Wills** now retired, was the Director of Music at Ely Cathedral, England from 1958 to 1990. He has broadcast, appeared on TV and made many recordings, and is a prolific composer for organ. Arthur Wills was appointed OBE in 1990. His memoirs have been published under the title *Full With Wills*. www.impulse-music.co.uk/arthurwills.htm

Todd **Wilson** is Professor of Organ at Indiana University's Jacobs School of Music and also serves as Organ Curator of the recently restored Norton Memorial Organ (E. M. Skinner, 1931) in Severance Hall, Cleveland, Ohio, USA.
http://en.wikipedia.org/wiki/Todd_Wilson

David **Wyld** has been involved in church music since the age of six and since 1997 has been the Managing Director of Henry Willis & Sons Ltd — the first MD since 1845 not to be a member of the Willis Family. www.willis-organs.com

Index

D

I

J

K

L

M

N

O

P

Q

R

S

T

U

V

W

Y

Fin